Radical Skepticism and
the Shadow of Doubt

ALSO AVAILABLE FROM BLOOMSBURY

The Bloomsbury Companion to Epistemology, edited by Andrew Cullison
Glimpse of Light, Stephen Mumford
Wittgenstein: The Crooked Roads, William Lyons

Radical Skepticism and the Shadow of Doubt

A Philosophical Dialogue

ELI HIRSCH

Bloomsbury Academic
An imprint of Bloomsbury Publishing Plc

B L O O M S B U R Y
LONDON · OXFORD · NEW YORK · NEW DELHI · SYDNEY

Bloomsbury Academic

An imprint of Bloomsbury Publishing Plc

50 Bedford Square	1385 Broadway
London	New York
WC1B 3DP	NY 10018
UK	USA

www.bloomsbury.com

**BLOOMSBURY and the Diana logo are trademarks of
Bloomsbury Publishing Plc**

First published 2018

© Eli Hirsch, 2018

Eli Hirsch has asserted his right under the Copyright, Designs and Patents Act, 1988, to be identified as the Author of this work.

British Library Cataloguing-in-Publication Data

A catalogue record for this book is available from the British Library.

ISBN:	HB:	978–1–3500–3384–9
	PB:	978–1–3500–3385–6
	ePDF:	978–1–3500–3383–2
	ePub:	978–1–3500–3387–0

Library of Congress Cataloging-in-Publication Data

A catalog record for this book is available from the Library of Congress.

Cover image © Irene Martinez Costa
Cover design: Jose A. Bernat Bacete/Getty Images

Typeset by RefineCatch Limited, Bungay, Suffolk
Printed and bound in Great Britain

To find out more about our authors and books visit www.bloomsbury.com. Here you will find extracts, author interviews, details of forthcoming events and the option to sign up for our newsletters.

CONTENTS

Preface ix

Radical skepticism and the shadow of doubt:
   A philosophical dialogue 1

Characters, setting, announcement 3

Act I Vatol's anxiety 5

Introduction to Lev's question 6
The example of Vatol 14
Yitzhak's reaction to skepticism, and Williamson's 21
On the nature of this work 25
The "two-level" view of the impossibility of doubt 27
The meaning of "reasons" to doubt 30
Relationships between "doubt," "belief," "assertion," and
   "certainty" 35
Further connections between "doubt," "anxiety," and "knowledge" 47
Interlude: Waiting for Godot 51
A connection to Nagel's skepticism 55
Interlude: philosophy and comedy 63
A challenge to Lev's assumptions about epistemic anxiety 65

Act II Vatol and Us 69

The n-to-n+1 argument 70
A safety condition on belief 78
Interlude: memories of Berkeley 81
Pryor's epistemic principle 83

Distinction between one-level and two-level cases 89
Interlude: Talmudic connections 94
The "non-circularity" condition 99
Daniel's challenges to Yitzhak's view 103
Yitzhak's stringent response to "entering a loop" 107
Yitzhak's Austinian answer to the problem of dreams 111
Interlude: finding an "eitzah" 129
Summary 131
Three additional questions 133
Lev's disagreement with Yitzhak 138

Act III The Impossibility of Doubt 143

Lev's past epistemic anxiety 143
Interlude: memories from Yeshiva 148
Lev's first argument for the impossibility of doubt 152
The first premise of Lev's first argument 159
A question about valuing one's life on the basis of probabilities 167
A comparison of Lev's position with Kant's and Wittgenstein's 172
Interlude: Yitzhak's tale 177
Lev's second argument 179
The meaning of "having a self" 188
Interlude: Yitzhak's pride and shame 196
Relationship between the notions of "self" and "identification" 198
Broughton's suggestion that Hume did not identify with his belief in
    an external reality 203
Lev's epistemic attitude 210

Notes 221
Glossary 227
References 228
Index 233

For Pam

PREFACE

Some philosophers are familiar with this book under the title "Epistemology Noir: A Philosophical Dialogue/Play on Skepticism about External Reality," which was its title for an extended period of time when I had it on my home page. Although for various reasons it seemed desirable to change the title, readers can be assured that the book's noir-ness is intact and it remains a dialogue-play. It obviously has a lot more philosophy than a typical play, but it also has a lot more non-philosophical action than a typical dialogue. The hope is that the different aspects of this book, the pure philosophy and the rest, fit together to offer a novel perspective on how we might talk about skepticism.

I was helped by a number of people in arriving at the ideas in this book. Many years ago Dean Kolitch and I spent endless, endless hours talking about Cartesian skepticism, and the general spirit and mood of those talks haunt this work. I take responsibility, however, for any mistakes in here about whether the world exists.

Philosophical discussions with Berislav Marušić helped me greatly as I was developing my ideas. Beri read and critiqued every page of successive drafts of the book, for which I am enormously appreciative. I am also exceedingly grateful to Jennifer Smalligan Marušić and Dan Korman for detailed comments on the entire work.

For comments on parts of the work, I give sincere thanks to Georges Dicker, Matti Eklund, Billy Flesch, Eugene Goodheart,

Pamela Hirsch, Matthias Jenny, Adam Leite, Miriam Schoenfield, and Palle Yourgrau.

And very special thanks to David Shatz for help with transliterations.

This book evolved over a number of years from several talks and papers with which many people helped me, most especially Georges Dicker and Beri Marušić, as well as Jonathan Adler, Arudra Barura, Matti Eklund, Pamela Hirsch, Tom Kelly, Dan Korman, Adam Leite, Matt McGrath, Abe Roth, Jerry Samet, Ted Sider, Tim Williamson, Palle Yourgrau, and audiences at the philosophy department at Indiana University, at the Center for Philosophic Exchange at SUNY Brockport, and at the philosophy department at the University of Vermont.

I am greatly indebted to Jed Lewinsohn for helping me to find the right venue for this book. And Coleen Coalter at Bloomsbury Press provided exactly the venue that I wanted, for which I am very grateful.

Above all else, I thank Pam, Dena, and Suzanna for helping always to keep sanity within sight.

RADICAL SKEPTICISM AND THE SHADOW OF DOUBT: A PHILOSOPHICAL DIALOGUE

Characters, setting, announcement

Act I. Vatol's Anxiety
Act II. Vatol and Us
Act III. The Impossibility of Doubt

The characters are Lev, Yitzhak, and Daniel, three aging philosophy professors who occasionally return to Yeshiva to study Talmud.

The setting is one of the bathrooms of a certain Yeshiva in New York City, where they have repaired in order to clear up some matters.

Opening Announcement
This work revolves around three propositions: (a) I have reason to doubt external reality (this proposition is explained in I and debated extensively in II). (b) Nevertheless, it is (metaphysically) impossible, insofar as I am a self-conscious and sane being, for me to doubt that I have meaningfully interacted with other beings (this proposition is introduced in I and debated in III). (c) I am therefore subject to a distinctive form of epistemic anxiety, the object of

which cannot possibly be faced or literalistically expressed (this proposition is discussed in I and in the final sections of III). The somewhat unorthodox style of the work is for the author associated in some ways with its content (see the section in I "on the nature of this work").

Act I

Vatol's Anxiety

[*Yitzhak, Daniel, and Lev entering the bathroom.*]

Yitzhak   . . . Yeah, maybe you're right. Maybe I lost it a little. But did you hear what this kid was saying? He was actually arguing that *tenai le-mafrea* should be viewed as a case of backwards causality.*

Daniel   You could have been more courteous, Yitzhak.

Yitzhak   I said to him, "Who the hell are you, a rabbinic reincarnation of Feynman?"

Daniel   Yes, Richard Feynman's picture of particles moving backwards in time. But you could have been more courteous. He is, after all, a student in this Yeshiva, we are merely visitors and guests . . . But let's put that aside. Lev has asked us in here to discuss something related to philosophy.

Lev   You must please pardon my somewhat uneasy English. I am still in the process of retrieving my American tongue.

---

* A *tenai le-mafrea* is a retroactive condition on a transaction, for example, the sale of an object may be valid at the present time on the condition that it is paid for at a certain later time. See, e.g., Kiddushin 60. (Casual Talmudic references are briefly explained at the bottom of the page; occasionally, more extended explanations are given in the text.)

Daniel   I'm sure it will improve as you go along. We could speak Hebrew or Yiddish with some difficulty, as the three of us sometimes did years ago when we first met at Berkeley, but that's not necessary. So what is on your mind, Lev?

Introduction to Lev's question

Lev   You had said, Daniel—this was upon my recent arrival from France—that in our reading group we shall do Descartes's Meditations.

Daniel   Yes, and you suggested, somewhat to my bafflement, that we combine this with discussion of the works of Thomas Nagel and Paul Feyerabend.

Lev   Daniel, I resist to go back to thinking about the Meditations. Such thoughts of course arouse feelings of anxiety and disorientation . . . *Ich mein* [I mean] . . . feelings which are against sanity.[1] The Cartesian reflection is in this respect like reflection about death. Of course one must not hide from these reflections.

The Cartesian reflection, if I may put it, is in essence this: I could possibly have been phenomenologically just as I am, throughout my entire existence, and yet completely deluded about the existence of all of the external facts that give meaning to my life. That would have been my situation if I had been deluded by Descartes' demon, or in the au courant image—Yes?—if I had been a brain in a vat. It is the possibility of being utterly alone in this way that, if a person thinks seriously and honestly about it, threatens sanity.

It is certain that other philosophers must react this way to the Cartesian reflection. Yes? Though I can point to very few places where philosophers are willing to admit to having such experiences ...

Yitzhak You know, you're a real *tummler*, my friend.

Daniel Hold on, Yitz, let's hear what he is saying.

Yitzhak There are people all over the world who, for one reason or another, are actually abandoned to horrible solitude and loneliness. They don't have time for Lev's so-called "anxiety" about Descartes' *Meditations*.

Daniel That's neither here nor there ...

Lev Yitzhak ... *Ich mein* ...

Yitzhak You know what you should do, Lev? You should have a "Rabbi Lonely Hearts" column for people who are lonely because they doubt that the world exists.

Daniel Listen, Lev, you mention two large topics, death and skepticism. Do you want to talk about both of them now? You know we have a limited amount of time here.

Lev Then I will stay with epistemology. But I think the topics are deeply related.

Daniel Sufficient unto each day the misery thereof, yes?

Yitzhak *Ein mearvin simcha be-simcha**

---

* The principle in Jewish law that one does not add one celebration to another e.g., one does not get married on a holiday. (Yerushalmi, Moed Katan 1:7).

Daniel   So, Lev. You said you don't find many philosophers who reveal that they react to the Cartesian reflection as you do. I suppose that two philosophers who may reveal this are Descartes and Hume? At various points early in the Meditations, especially at the beginning of the second Meditation, Descartes seems to be struggling to maintain his sanity, though perhaps this is intended by him only as a dialectical exercise.[2] And there is of course Hume's famous remark about the "melancholy and delirium" that results from his skepticism, and his bitter antidote of "carelessness and inattention."[3] It seems that these two great philosophers may perhaps convey that they were made anxious by their doubts

Lev   First, Daniel, I am not saying that I am made anxious by *doubts*. I am made anxious if I reflect deeply on the metaphysical possibility of my being utterly deluded about everything that matters to me. What I am affirming is that apart from Hume, and perhaps Descartes, and I would include Thomas Nagel, and of course Wittgenstein, I do not detect clear indications in many other philosophers ...

Yitzhak   Wait a minute! You're not made anxious by *doubts*? So what's making you anxious about the Cartesian reflection, if not doubts?

Lev   Doubt of that sort is not a possibility.

Yitzhak   I don't understand what you're talking about.

Daniel   Let's slow this down. You seem to be saying two things, Lev: first, that the Cartesian reflection cannot lead you to doubt, and second, that the Cartesian reflection induces a special kind of epistemic anxiety in you. The first claim is familiar, in both recent and older literature. In his lectures on naturalism Peter Strawson said that the only answer to skepticism is that we cannot possibly doubt that there is an external reality.[4] Nagel says much the same thing.[5] As do various other recent writers.

Lev   At one point in the *Investigations* the interlocutor says, "Isn't it that you are shutting your eyes in the face of doubt?" And Wittgenstein answers, "They are shut."[6]

Yitzhak   Brilliant! *Moirewdik*! What genius! "They are shut."

Daniel   In any case, the idea that doubt of the relevant sort is not possible is a familiar idea. The idea seems to be famously expressed at various points by Hume, when he says that our nature invariably overcomes our reason. So your first claim need not puzzle us. But your two claims together must of course invite Yitzhak's question, "What is making you anxious, if not doubt?"

Lev   Daniel and Yitzhak. I did, when I was younger, think that it was doubt that was making me anxious. I never told either of you this, but when the three of us were at Berkeley I once went to see a psychiatrist at the health center.

Yitzhak   In the University Hospital?

Lev   Yes.

Daniel   I do vaguely recall some difficult moments. There was an episode with peyote. Or was that Yitz? And at some point you left Berkeley rather abruptly and finished your thesis while in France.

Lev   I told the psychiatrist that I lived in a panic because I doubted that there was a world outside my consciousness.

Daniel   Ah.

Yitzhak   You actually told that to a psychiatrist? Was he Jewish?

Lev   He was a very clever Chinese man. He said an interesting thing to me. He requested if I always felt the same degree of anxiety. I told him no, sometimes it was worse. He said, then our job would be to try to understand why it is worse some times than other times.

Yitzhak   Well, the answer, given what you've said, is that it's worse when you think about it, when you reflect on it seriously and honestly, as you put it.

Daniel   But obviously that wasn't what he was talking about. He must have meant that some problems in your personal life were causing you to experience anxiety that you then projected onto this famous philosophical issue. But I gather that didn't go anywhere for you?

Lev   Daniel and Yitzhak. Here is a joke that I believe I once made up myself. A man goes to his session with his psychoanalyst. The psychoanalyst requests how he is doing. The man says, "I am falling apart. I had some medical tests. I have an inoperable tumor in my spine and I will be completely paralyzed within a year." The psychoanalyst says, "What does that remind you of?"

Daniel   Ah . . . Explanations have to come to an end.

Yitzhak   The sooner the better.

Daniel   But, *her zich ein* [listen], Lev, you *are* giving an explanation. You are saying that the Cartesian reflection produces your anxiety. And you say, furthermore, that other philosophers surely have the same experience. And yet the experience does not come out of doubting, you say. So it may appear that your explanation of your anxiety makes no sense.

Yitzhak   No sense at all! What is the anxiety *about*?

Daniel   Yes, are you able to answer that? If you are not doubting that you are meaningfully connected to an external world, about what are you anxious?

Lev   I cannot explain this in words. I believe it is an essential part of this experience that its content cannot be put into ordinary words. By the by, Daniel, you have mentioned that Hume said he could not doubt, yet he also said his philosophical reflections made him anxious.

Daniel   Ah ... That is interesting. So perhaps this peculiar epistemic anxiety, not anchored in doubt, was felt by Hume ...

Lev   And every other philosopher who engages in the Cartesian reflection ... at least deep down. Whether they face it or not.

Yitzhak   Every other philosopher? Are you joking?

Daniel   Let's put aside for the moment who does and who does not have this experience. We want to understand what the experience is in Lev's case.

Yitzhak   You know, Lev, I think what you are is what William James called a "diabolical mystic," a mystic of the dark side.[7] I think he also called such people deranged.

Daniel It's interesting that you refer to James, to his profound book *The Varieties of Religious Experience*. I'm reminded of a famous distinction James makes in that book, between the "healthy-minded" and the "sick souls."[8] He himself was of course a big fan of the latter. This is a distinction that one might usefully apply within epistemology. It's striking that some philosophers are troubled by the Cartesian reflection and some are not—though Lev seems to want to say that all really are troubled "deep down."

Lev I believe James contended that everyone is really sick-souled deep down.

Daniel Yes? I didn't think so. I don't think I saw that in James. In any case, we might distinguish between sick-souled epistemology and healthy-minded epistemology. Lev here is evidently a sick-souled epistemologist, and you, Yitzhak, are a healthy-minded epistemologist, as is your paragon Williamson, who dismisses what he calls "the disease" of skepticism.[9]

Yitzhak Lev, my sick-souled dear old friend, let me ask you one thing, since we're also speaking of Descartes. He said that, with respect to his problem, the solution was God. I don't really understand yet what your problem is, but couldn't God be the solution to it?

Lev God is irrelevant. If there is God, God too must face the Cartesian reflection just like us.

Daniel If there is God?

Yitzhak That even God can feel lost and abandoned—there are a lot of things like that in Kabbalah. But of course that has nothing to do with the Cartesian reflection. God is omniscient.

Lev Do you think you understand what that means, Yitzhak? What I am saying is that any conceivable being that literally has a subjective consciousness and is rational must be affected as we are by the Cartesian reflection.

Daniel Listen, *kinder* [children], let's get off this. Our plan wasn't to talk about the philosophy of religion. Certainly in the case of God we have nothing but analogies. And silence. *Seyag le-chochmah shtikah*: "The safeguard of wisdom is silence."[10]

Yitzhak *Reishis chochma yir'as Hashem* : "The beginning of wisdom is the fear of God."[11]

Lev *Va-yaster moshe panav ki yarei me-habit el ha-Elokim*: "Mosheh hid his face, for he was afraid to look upon God."[12] . . . *Ich mein* . . . The imperative to face what cannot possibly be faced . . .

Yitzhak What is this *meshugena* talking about?

Daniel I don't know. I'm beginning to wonder myself.

Lev I do not think I am putting things as I want to.

Daniel Good. Good. I want to say, Lev, that listening to some of the things you say, I do feel I have a sense of how you are reacting to the Cartesian reflection. And I think that this can be put in plain language. Do you want to hear?

Lev Of course. Please, Daniel.

Daniel Part of your reaction is that you think there is reason to doubt. But you realize that it is impossible to doubt. There is therefore a conflict, a clash, between your sense that you ought rationally to doubt and your inability to doubt. It is that clash that generates your anxiety.

Lev Thank you, Daniel. I am thinking that is much helpful. *Ich mein*, certainly the conflict you mention is in the heart of the matter. But I am thinking this still does not allow me to answer Yitzhak's question in plain, literal language. *Ich mein*, there is still no intelligible answer to the question, "What are you anxious *about*?" There is an example I am thinking about, a kind of thought-experiment, that I believe can make some of the issues here more vivid.

Daniel Good, let's hear it.

Yitzhak *Luz heren!*

The example of Vatol

Lev My thought experiment: I am supposing a world in which there are many normal people and also many vat-people, you understand that these are people who spend their entire lives as brains-in-vats not knowing that they are really hallucinating. I am imagining that Vatol is one of the normal people in this world. I am imagining that when he is growing up Vatol finds out about the vat-people as in ordinary ways. You understand that he first hears something about it when he is little—yes?—then he is given much more details at home and in school when he is growing up. You understand that there are vat-people in books, and magazine articles, and in movies. In Vatol's neighborhood he sees a building, let us suppose, the Central Committee on Vatting.

Yitzhak   I hope Cheney is not on it!

Lev   Vatol understands that this reality of numerous vat-people began a few years before his own birth.

Yitzhak   Why would there be a practice of creating vat-people?

Lev   That I do not know. But you must imagine this somehow.

Daniel   How about like this? The reason, very schematically, was that there had eventually accumulated in laboratories around the planet billions of fertilized ova in vitro, and when an electromagnetic alteration in the atmosphere threatened to destroy all of them, it was decided by an international body that, the technology being available, it would be best to make vat-people out of those fertilized ova.

Yitzhak   *Meshuga!*

Lev   Thank you, Daniel! Yes, that can be our imagining. Now I am hoping that even if you say that we, in our actual situation, have no reason to feel troubled by the fact that we might possibly have been brains in vats, you will agree that Vatol does have reason to feel troubled.

Daniel   I agree. What about you, Yitzhak?

Yitzhak   That Vatol has reason to be troubled about whether he is a vat-person? Yeah, I think I agree with that.

Lev   I want you to now imagine that *you* are Vatol.

Yitzhak   Uh, oh. Hang on, people, we may be approaching a capillary of darkness.

Daniel   A capillary of darkness . . . Conrad?

Yitzhak   You know, when the logical positivist Schlick was shot to death by one of his students? He was murmuring something as he lay dying. When they got close they could hear him saying, "The vagueness, the vagueness—"

Daniel   Okay, very good. Go on, Lev.

Lev   Yes. Yes . . . I want you to now imagine that *you* are Vatol. And my challenge is for you to be explaining to me in plain language what is troubling you. I will now add a little twist on this: Suppose that you were informed when you were little that you have a brother who is one of the vat-people.

Yitzhak   Wait a minute! Is this whole thing really about your crazy relationship with your brother?

Daniel   Come on, *sha*, Yitzhak.

Lev   . . . Let us suppose further that today a technological test was performed in which an electromagnetic "phone" hookup—a hookup, yes?—is established between you and your envatted brother. I am imagining that for some obscure reasons, perhaps something having to do with technological symmetry, your brother's hallucinations have been arranged to make him believe that he is being hooked up to his envatted brother, that *you* are a vat-person.

Daniel   This will be an amazingly strange conversation! Both you and your brother believing that the other's descriptions of his life are completely delusive.

Lev   Yes, yes, exactly! Each believes that the other is completely deluded about his life. I am now putting to you this question: How will you feel when you get off the phone?

Yitzhak   Well, at least, whether I'm a vat-person or not, I spoke to my brother.

Daniel   I think that is a trivial mistake, Yitz. You cannot think, "Well, even if I'm envatted, at least I've had contact with my brother." That would be absurd. You have no reason to think that, if you are envatted, you really have a brother or really have spoken to anyone.

Yitzhak   Right, right. Sorry for that blunder.

Daniel   In fact, it would be equally absurd for Vatol to say, "Well, at least I know that some vat exists." When we agreed a moment ago that Vatol has reason to be troubled about whether he is a vat-person what that really meant was that he has reason to doubt all of his experiences. When we imagine Vatol worrying, "Maybe I'm a vat-person," that's just an especially vivid form of the worry, "Maybe it's all just a hallucination, maybe there is nothing about external reality that I know."

Lev   Yes, as in Descartes.

Yitzhak   Right, right.

Lev   Yes, yes! So I am asking: How will you *feel* when you get off the phone?

Daniel   I think it is clear that in these circumstances one will feel extremely troubled and bewildered. One might feel this even if one is not a philosopher, but must certainly feel it if one is a philosopher.

Lev   Yes, yes, excellent! And my challenge to you is to tell me what you are troubled *about*.

Daniel   Well, of course you may feel bad for your brother and the other vat-people, but I assume that's not what we're talking about. I assume we are talking about a feeling of anxiety that I will initially want to express by saying, "Maybe *I* am a vat-person!"

Lev   Yes, yes, Daniel, that is what you will be pushed towards saying: "Maybe I am a vat-person."

Daniel   But, if by saying that, I am saying that I don't believe that I am not a vat-person, I cannot really mean it, at least if we are now agreeing with those many philosophers who said that doubting the reality of the external world is not a possibility. I take it, that is your puzzle, Lev. If I can't really doubt that I'm a normal person, what am I really anxious about?

Lev   Yes, thank you, Daniel! That is what is puzzling!

Yitzhak   Wait a minute. Hume and these other guys, when they say doubt is impossible, they would apply that to someone like Vatol?

Daniel   What are you asking, Yitz? These philosophers claim that we have reason to doubt, that Reason supports doubting, as Hume put it, but still, they say, we can't possibly doubt. Why would it not be the same for Vatol?

Yitzhak   If there is reason to doubt, why claim that it is impossible to doubt? Does anyone have an argument for that claim?

Lev   I believe I have an argument, or two arguments. I can give them to you.

Daniel   Good, good, you will present those arguments to us later, Lev. In Hume and probably Nagel the argument is simply that our "nature" makes it impossible for us to have that kind of doubt. But let's come back to that later. It's interesting to see where this will go if we do agree with those philosophers and assume that it's impossible to doubt even if there is reason to doubt. Let that be our assumption for now, the impossibility-of-doubt assumption.

Lev   Yes, we will come back to it. But permit me to emphasize now that your perspective as Vatol must be considered in a manner that is concrete and vivid. From your view as Vatol you are possessing a perfectly normal life—you grew from being little, you arrived at friends, you became married, you made children—a perfectly normal life—yes?—but in this life there was also the news about the vat-people, and then your brother, and the conversation with him. You of course must be remembering vividly many of the people and events in your life. You will talk to your philosopher friends of your epistemic situation—yes?—of the very situation we are now discussing, and when you are talking to your friends of course you will be believing that your friends exist. Therefore I want you to tell me now what you would tell your friends. Tell me what is troubling you. But please do not tell me that you do not believe that you have really lived a normal human life, *Ich mein,* a life outside of a vat. That would be a falsehood.

Daniel   Yes, that would be a falsehood, at least given the assumption that we are now making about the impossibility of doubting external reality.

Yitzhak   Well, can't I feel troubled by the fact that I have reason to doubt? That's what we're assuming, right? And since I have reason to doubt, even though I don't doubt, I don't have *knowledge*, at least on many views of what's required for knowledge. Can't that trouble me?

Lev   No! Why should that be a trouble for you? What do you care about whether you have reason to doubt, or about whether you have knowledge? You *do not* doubt. That is now our assumption. Yes? So you are saying to yourself, "Of course I am in contact with an external world. I am a human being, living a normal human life. I am not a brain in a vat." Having said that to yourself, what are you being anxious about? But you *will* be anxious, for sure you will be anxious!

Yitzhak   Okay, I begin to see what you're driving at. Maybe I would feel intellectually troubled and puzzled by my epistemic situation, in the way that I might feel troubled by not being able to understand how to resolve the liar's paradox. Or maybe I would feel a bit intellectually deflated if I thought that beliefs that I can't possibly get rid of are not rational or not virtuous in Ernie Sosa's sense.[13] But why would I feel *anxious*? What am I anxious *about* if I'm not doubting? It's as if I'm experiencing the anxiety of doubt, but without doubting. So it's possible that you're trying to ask a good question, Lev.

Lev   Yes, Yitzhak. Like experiencing the anxiety of doubt, but without doubting.

Daniel   So that is Lev's paradox. The anxiety of doubt, but without doubting. And therefore no way of explaining—at least not in plain language—what the anxiety is about.

Yitzhak   Lev's paradox. I like that. Or should it be the paradox of Lev, like the paradox of the heap? Lev himself is the paradox . . . But what exactly is the paradox? People have anxiety attacks all the time that they can't explain . . . But I guess this is different . . .

Daniel   Yes, it seems very different. If I am Vatol I realize that I have reason to doubt. And therefore I have reason to be anxious. But I cannot doubt, that is our assumption. Yet the anxiety remains. In a sense I do understand very well what is making me anxious, but I am somehow debarred from saying it, from thinking it.

Lev   Yes, Daniel. Thank you. Debarred from thinking it. Yes.

Yitzhak   "Debarred from thinking it"? I don't know if I understand what that means. I don't know. Maybe.

Yitzhak's reaction to skepticism, and Williamson's

Daniel   Okay. Good. We'll talk more about this . . . But let me first ask you something, Yitz. You agree that in Vatol's situation you would be anxious. That may be, you said, because you would actually doubt in that situation. So you do agree—don't you?—that if you doubted the reality of the external world that would make you anxious.

Yitzhak   Well, yes, of course. Obviously! If I doubted that I have ever really known anybody, spoken to anybody? If I doubted that I really grew up with my parents and brothers and sisters. Everything that has happened since. My wife, my kids . . . And you guys. We went to different Yeshivas, Lev in France, until we met in Berkeley doing philosophy, Danny already a professor. And now we meet sometimes in the Yeshiva to learn again.* If I doubted that we three band of brothers are here, on this day, in this bathroom, in this Yeshiva, in New York City, standing in front of these toilet bowls, unwilling to give ground . . . If I doubted the reality of my family, my friends, doubted that I ever lived a human life at all? Of course I would be terrified out of my mind. Obviously.

Daniel   But Timothy Williamson does not think this.

Yitzhak   What do you mean?

Daniel   Williamson thinks that if he doubted external reality this would barely affect him.

Yitzhak   Where do you see this?

Daniel   In his book "The Philosophy of Philosophy" Williamson asks why it would matter if we doubted external reality. And his answer is that this might affect our altruism.[14]

Yitzhak   Yeah. Yeah, I vaguely remember that now. It's a tiny passage in the book. But, come on, he doesn't say that altruism is the *only* thing that would be affected by such doubts.

---

* In the Yeshiva world "learn" is short for "learn Torah," the latter meaning, "study the Talmud."

Daniel   I realize that. But listen to this, Yitz. Williamson dedicates the book to his three children. He mentions each of them by name! Then inside the book when he asks why skepticism would matter, what he hits on is altruism. If you are a brain in a vat then your wish to love and be loved by your children is denied. Isn't that the most obvious and important kind of example of why it makes a practical difference whether you're a brain in a vat?

Yitzhak   Yeah. Maybe he wanted to mention something more directly related to actions. I don't know. But look, it has to be understood that Lev here, with his epistemology noir, is off on a weird track of his own. People who talk about skepticism just aren't thinking about it in those terms. No one is talking about *anxiety*. For someone like Williamson epistemology is a purely intellectual exercise. He probably doesn't want to bring any personal baggage into it. Imagine a surgeon who has to operate on his child. He tries to forget that personal side of it in order to do his business better.

Lev   Williamson said, "Must do better."[15] Samuel Beckett said, "Try again, fail again, fail better."[16]

Yitzhak   I sense that the course of analytic epistemology is making Lev despair about the future of pessimism.

Daniel   But suppose someone asks the surgeon during the surgery why it would be so bad to fail. He doesn't answer that it's because it will raise his insurance.

Yitzhak   Yeah. All right.

Lev   Daniel's point is that while Williamson is dismissing the "disease of skepticism" he seems to have no understanding, no understanding at all of what it would be like to suffer from that "disease."

Yitzhak   Yeah, I see the point. I do. Listen, who's this? "When Williamson speaks about skepticism he doesn't have any real understanding of the that-about-which-he-is-speaking about which he is speaking." It starts with an "h" and ends with an "r." Not Hitler.

Daniel   But, seriously, Yitz, do you think this is a . . .

Yitzhak   And not Himmler.

Daniel   . . . a serious complaint against Williamson?

Yitzhak   I don't know . . . No, I don't really think so. Maybe Williamson does slip up a little bit in singling out altruism as a loss in skepticism. But it has no adverse effect at all on his overall epistemological enterprise.

Lev   I do not want to press you, Yitzhak. I appreciate how much you admire Williamson. But do you not see that it is because Williamson has given no serious thought to what it would be like to doubt external reality that he assumes that philosophers have actually suffered from what he calls the disease of skepticism? He believes philosophers such as Russell who say that they doubt external reality, when any serious thought about what such doubt must mean would have shown him, as it even showed Moore, that none of these philosophers actually doubted.[17] Would you not say therefore that

Williamson's remark about altruism displays an extraordinary deficiency in his approach to epistemology?

Yitzhak   No! I would not say that! I've already answered the question. Williamson probably didn't give a moment's thought to that little remark about altruism. It simply plays no significant role in his overall enterprise.

Lev   His enterprise.

Yitzhak   Yeah. His enterprise.

Daniel   Okay. Good. Then let's return to what we were talking about . . .

On the nature of this work

Yitzhak   Wait a second, Danny. Maybe this is a bit crazy, but I want to try something. I want to talk a little bit about what Hirsch had in mind in casting us in these peculiar roles.

Daniel   No! You can't do that, Yitzhak! That's not a possibility! Don't you see how incoherent that is?

Yitzhak   Let me try it just for a minute. My main question is what is this business of a "dialogue/play" instead of just a traditional philosophical dialogue. Why inject distractions from the central epistemological issues we're trying to discuss? Why all the tomfoolery: the insults, jokes, reminiscences that we're constantly involved in? And why all the Jewish Talmudic stuff mixed in? What's the point of all of that?

Lev   I believe, Yitzhak, that our author aspires to show what is said. To show, not merely to tell.

Yitzhak   To show? I don't know what you're talking about.

Lev   For example, we are three occasional Talmud students, three Talmudist-manqués—yes?—in a bathroom discussing philosophy. This is as in an Edward Albee play in which people suddenly undress while they continue to sit on a sofa calmly discussing their taxes.

Yitzhak   Three naked Talmudists in a bathroom discussing philosophy, maybe one of them on the toilet. So it could have been worse.

Lev   I will remain here leaning against the sink. If necessary, I will remove my jacket, but no more.

Yitzhak   So we're characters in Absurdist Theater? Is that it?

Lev   Showing absurdity, yes, that I think is part of it. But I conjecture that more than this our author thinks that a certain kind of religious sensibility, *Ich mein*, not every kind, but a certain kind, perhaps with a philosophical bent, such as that shown by our characters in this work, may react to philosophical issues of belief and doubt with a sense of existential urgency—yes?—a sense of existential urgency less likely to be found in other people. Would you not agree with that, Yitzhak?

Yitzhak   Do I agree with that? No, I don't think so. I don't think I'm aware of any evidence for that. But I'm really afraid that if I start criticizing Hirsch for being self-indulgent in this work, this whole thing will go up in smoke, like in one of those science fiction stories about time-travel, where if you try to change the present, the universe with you in it is retroactively annihilated.

Lev *Chas ve-shalom.* [Heaven forbid]

Yitzhak In any case, here's an announcement I want to make to our readers. As for all the Jewish Talmudic stuff, if you don't get it, it's fine to skim or skip it; that won't prevent you from following the rest. In fact, all of the sections marked as "interlude" can be skipped by anyone who wants something more closely resembling a standard philosophical dialogue.

Lev Yet, will something then be lost, something that is somehow connected to the epistemological issues?

Daniel Listen! I have the role of moderator in this discussion! And I insist that we not wander off incoherently into another dimension of discourse. Is that understood?

Yitzhak Okay. Okay.

Lev We possess your back, Daniel.

The "two-level" view of the impossibility of doubt

Daniel Okay. Good. Then let's return to what we were talking about. We're assuming for now the impossibility-of-doubt view found in a number of philosophers. Lev has promised to present us with an argument for this view. But I want to mention that some of these philosophers have a "two-level" view of this impossibility. At the level of ordinary life we cannot doubt, but at the level of philosophical reflection about skepticism, we do doubt. This view is clearly in Strawson and Nagel, whom we've cited earlier. Janet Broughton applies it to Hume.[18] If this view is correct it seems that Vatol may have no difficulty explaining what he is anxious about. He can appeal to his doubting at the reflective level.

Lev   I wish you to explain to me how this works, Daniel. When Vatol's philosopher-level engages in the enterprise of doubting it feels anxiety? No? So the ordinary-person level feels anxious while not doubting because the philosopher-level doubts while not feeling anxious?

Daniel   I see. Okay. Well, I really have no idea how to answer your question. As Yitz just remarked, it seems that no one talks about these things in terms of skeptical anxiety.

Lev   Perhaps Thomas Nagel. He is close.

Daniel   Yes? Okay, I may see the connection. I hope we can come back to that. But my point right now is that when you explain to us why you think doubt is impossible I hope you will address this two-level position.

Lev   I am familiar with the position, Daniel. I believe it contains a deep distortion. I will be happy to address it.

Yitzhak   I really don't know what to say about any of this. But there is something intuitively right about the two-level formulation. If I am Vatol, maybe I don't doubt at the level at which I go about my life, but deep down I must doubt.

Lev   Are you sure that if you go that far down deep, Yitzhak, there is still an "I" to be found there?

Yitzhak   What do you mean?

Lev   I mean that with regard to the kind of doubt we are discussing, it may be that where I am doubt is not, and where doubt is I am not.

Daniel   Epicurus's formulation about death.[19]

Lev   Yes, truths as reassuring here as there. But death is not our topic.

Yitzhak   What do you mean? It's not reassuring?

Lev   Is it?

Yitzhak   I don't really know what you're talking about. You think Epicurus's reassurance is stupid?

Lev   Some ideas do not attain the status of stupidity. Is dishonesty a form of stupidity?

Yitzhak   I don't know what the hell you're talking about.

Daniel   Okay! Okay! Let's keep on track, please! Death is not our topic.

Yitzhak   Are you sure of that, Danny?

Daniel   Come on, Yitz. Let's try to stay on track. Okay. We're going to come back to talk more about the impossibility-of-doubt position.*

The meaning of "reasons" to doubt

Daniel (continuing)   But there are a couple of other things that we first have to clear up. Here's an immediate thing. When we say—and I think the three of us agree on this—that Vatol has reason to doubt, we don't just mean that he has some prima facie reason to doubt that is trumped by a stronger reason not to doubt. We mean that, all things considered, he has reason to doubt. I think that's clearly what we have in mind. Do I hear any objections to that? No? Good, good. Now here is another point . . .

Yitzhak   But there is a complication to mention about this. A distinction is sometimes made between "epistemic" or "evidential" reasons to believe or doubt and "pragmatic" reasons.[20] A rough sense of the distinction as it's often understood is this: only epistemic reasons can be the basis for knowledge claims. I think for our purposes a better formulation might be something like this: A pragmatic reason to believe is in the first instance a reason to *want* to believe; if this can actually generate a reason to believe, the reason to believe is derivative of the reason to want to believe. An epistemic reason to believe is not derivative of a reason to want to believe.

---

* That position is the topic of act III. Doubting "deep down" is discussed on pp. 204 ff.

Maybe that won't cover every example. Marušić holds that a pragmatic reason to believe that you're going to do something can derive from having a reason to *intend* to do it.[21] We could try to accommodate Marušić's view by putting it like this: A pragmatic reason to believe a proposition p is a reason to believe that is derivative of there being a reason for some other propositional attitude towards p, some attitude other than believing, whether this be the attitude of wanting to believe or the attitude of intending. I think this is probably good enough for our purposes. Now, it seems immediately obvious that if we hold there can be such a thing as pragmatic reasons to believe, then Vatol has an abundance of such reasons to believe in an external reality. But I take it that we're talking about epistemic reasons when we say that he has reason to doubt. And we're assuming that, this being the case, he has reason to feel anxious. I would be tempted to say that he's anxious because deep down he really doubts. But Lev denies that, and thinks that the anxiety is therefore a puzzle.

Lev   It is a puzzle to say what the object of the anxiety is.

Daniel   Yes, very good. Let's be clear, then, that when we talk about reasons we mean always epistemic reasons. Maybe we will have to say more about that later. And I wanted to mention another thing. It has to be noted that we are ignoring Putnam's view that even the vat-people are not deceived,[22] because we . . .

Yitzhak   Duly noted.

Daniel   . . . because we find that approach unpersuasive.

Yitzhak   Duly noted.

Lev   Having demonstrated the existence of external reality, why did Putnam not also present a proof of the existence of God, and of the immortality of the soul?

Yitzhak   Uh, oh. Lev's getting a little testy!

Lev   Putnam's argument is most terrible on beliefs about other people. If I am a vat-person then, for Putnam, I believe truly that "I discourse with other people who have feelings and thoughts about me." Vatol, if he is smart, will not be anxious? How could this argument be honest and serious?

Daniel   I think Lev makes a good point. The attraction of a view like Putnam's, or various other verificationist or "transcendental" arguments that the fantasy that I am suffering from radical deception is incoherent, that this is not even an intelligible possibility—the attraction of such views must certainly be dampened by considering what you would say in Vatol's situation.

Lev   Of course it is easy to see that Putnam's argument brings an absurd conclusion, but not so easy to see where the mistake is. We need to look at Kripke's idea of "picking out a property essentially."[23] Then we may see the fallacy in Putman's thought.

Daniel   Okay. Good, good. We won't go into any of those details, Lev, about which I don't think we're all agreed, but we're at least agreed to set Putnam's argument aside. Now here is another question. In this discussion do we have to take account of various contextualist positions? Or can we put that aside?

Lev   I believe, Daniel, that the only context that concerns us is the context of the Cartesian reflection. That is our context of utterance and our context of evaluation.[24] As regards people outside that context, our evaluation of their carelessness and inattention is forgiveness. As we forgive ourselves.

Yitzhak   Forgiveness won't be the right attitude on the view that inattention changes what are the "relevant alternatives" and therefore changes what it is reasonable to believe.[25]

Lev   You are saying, Yitzhak, that Vatol's carelessness and inattention to facts that gives reason to doubt might itself make a reason for him not to doubt but to believe?

Yitzhak   Yeah, that doesn't sound very good. Maybe that sort of view sounds better about "knowledge" than it does about "reasons to believe." I don't know. Then there is also the Fantl–McGrath view that seems to imply that differences in the stakes can alter the truth-values of sentences of the form "S has reason to believe (or doubt) p," but I'm not sure how this should work when p is the proposition that there is an external world.[26] Remember that we're always trying to talk about "epistemic reasons." In any case, I think what Lev said before is the right thing. Let's just stick to the context of reflecting on the skeptical problem.

Daniel   Good. So that will be understood. Let me ask something else. We've been talking about "reasons to believe or doubt." What about the concepts of "justified belief" and "rational belief"? How do we want to deal with those concepts? Do we take them to be definable in terms of "reasons to believe"? I'm inclined to think that is the case. But perhaps the safest course for us is to leave that open and try to carry on our conversation in terms of the concept of "reasons" to believe or doubt.

Yitzhak   There is one more thing. If I understand Nozick right, he said, to my absolute amazement, that even if we confine ourselves to the context of philosophical reflection, I can know that I'm really standing here speaking to you guys, but I can't know that I'm not really a brain in a vat who never speaks to anyone.[27] That makes absolutely no sense to me whatsoever . . .

Daniel   I think Kripke might agree with you.[28]

Yitzhak   . . . but when Bernard Williams reviewed Nozick's book he said that's one thing in the book he really liked.[29] Well, so it is in philosophy. I think a number of people have expressed agreement with Nozick on this. Now, I don't know if people also say this about reasons to believe, that, in the context of philosophical reflection, I have reason to believe that I'm really standing here talking to you guys, but I can't have reason to believe that I'm not really a brain in a vat who never speaks to anyone. I don't know if anyone says that. But let's be clear that when we talk in this discussion about having reason to believe "that there is an external reality" or "that I'm not a vat-person," what we're primarily talking about is having reason to believe the normal specific things that we believe about external reality, like that I'm really standing here talking to you guys. Apart from those specific beliefs such relatively abstract sentences as "I'm not a brain in a vat" or "There is an external reality" have little interest. If it somehow made sense to say—as it surely doesn't!—that

I have reason for the specific beliefs but not for those more abstract sentences, that would be good enough, to put it mildly—and absurdly.

Daniel   So I think you are saying that if one has reason to doubt that one is not a brain in a vat then one surely has reason to doubt the specific beliefs that matter in one's life. That does seem completely clear to me. We will assume agreement on this?

Relationships between "doubt," "belief," "assertion," and "certainty"

Daniel   (continuing) Okay. Good, good . . . But now a more serious question. We are assuming, for further discussion, that it is impossible to doubt that there is an external world. The expression "doubts that p" seems however to be ambiguous. In the *strong* sense to doubt that p is to not believe that p, that is, to lack a belief that p.

Yitzhak   The expression "does not believe that p" sometimes implies "believes that not-p." I don't know if that's really a correct literal use. Let's just stipulate that we will always use "does not believe that p" to mean nothing more than "lacks a belief that p."

Daniel   Good, good. We will follow that stipulation. So, I was saying, the strong sense of "doubts that p" implies "does not believe that p," that is, "lacks a belief that p." But it seems that there may be a weaker sense. It may seem that you can believe that p but "have some doubts." You can believe that p but not be fully confident, not be *certain.* In that kind of case it seems that you have some doubts that *p*; in that sense, you doubt that *p*, even though you believe that *p*. Now my question is this: When these philosophers say that it is impossible to doubt that there is an external reality, do they only mean that it's impossible to not believe, or do they mean that it's even impossible to have some doubts, to believe while not being certain? If they allow the possibility of belief without certainty, then it seems that Vatol can explain his anxiety by saying, "Maybe it's all a hallucination," meaning by this that he believes but is uncertain.

Yitzhak   Let's be very clear about something. It's one thing to say, "It may be that *p*," or "Maybe *p*," and a very different thing to say "It might have been the case that *p*." You can say, "It might have been the case that *p*, but it certainly isn't the case," whereas you obviously can't say, "It may be the case that *p*, but it certainly isn't the case." Of course Vatol will say, "It might have been the case that it's all a hallucination." But your question, Danny, is whether he can say, "It may be the case that it's all a hallucination," thereby expressing uncertainty.

Daniel   Exactly. My question is whether, according to the impossibility-of-doubt view, Vatol's belief is compatible with uncertainty, with saying that it may not be so.

Yitzhak   Yeah, yeah, Danny, that's a good question. I think we need to consider the connections suggested in Williamson between assertion and belief, and between assertion and certainty.[30] Suppose I assert, "Muttel Finkelstein still lives in Cleveland." It would seem clearly wrong for me to follow this up by saying, "though maybe he doesn't." The assertion "He lives in Cleveland, but maybe he doesn't" sounds almost as bad as the Moore-paradox assertion "He lives in Cleveland, but I don't believe it." It follows that there is no sense of the concept "doubting p" that permits you to assert "p, but I doubt it," since "I doubt it," even in the sense of "I have some doubts about it," implies "Maybe it's not so." If we take certainty that p to be basically equivalent to not judging "maybe not-p," it seems that a necessary condition for properly asserting something is that you're certain of it.[31] Now belief, as Williamson says, is in a sense the subjective counterpart of assertion. If you can't properly assert something without being certain of it, then you can't properly believe something without being certain of it. If you're not certain that p is true, then you can believe that p is probable—in that sense you can believe p "to a degree"—but you shouldn't believe p outright; you shouldn't believe it *simpliciter*.

Lev   As Descartes said at the end of Meditation 1. If you are not certain that there is an external reality, then you must suspend belief, though you can believe it is more likely than not.

Daniel   Yes, all of this is very good. But where exactly does it leave us with regard to Vatol? We are assuming that Vatol has reason to not believe, and that nevertheless he does believe. Suppose we now add the assumption that it is counter-normative to believe without being certain. What follows? Does it follow that he has reason to be certain because he believes, or that he has reason not to be certain because he has reason not to believe? And there is something else. Let's suppose that the right answer is that he has reason to be certain. It does not follow that he *is* certain. Perhaps he is uncertain even though he has reason to be certain, just as he believes even though he has reason not to believe. This would explain why he is anxious.

He is anxious because he is uncertain, because he judges, "Maybe it is all a hallucination." The assumption that this judgment is counter-normative is irrelevant. The point that Lev wants to make with the Vatol example is that in this example there is epistemic anxiety that cannot be explained in plain language. That was supposed to follow from the impossibility-of-doubt thesis. But it doesn't follow unless that thesis implies that it is not just counter-normative, but *impossible* for Vatol to be uncertain.

Yitzhak   Yes, I think that's right, Danny.

Lev   I am in agreement. For the example to work as I wish it to it must be supposed that it is *impossible* for Vatol to believe but be uncertain. Now I am actually not feeling sure that it ever makes good sense to talk of being uncertain while believing. But even if this should make good sense in some cases I wish to say that there are special problems in the case of believing that there is an external reality. What can it mean to believe without being certain? It seems this must mean to believe without believing to the *highest* degree. But my feeling is that for the belief in external reality there can be no degrees of belief. Philosophers have talked of betting propensities as determining degrees of belief. What kind of bet can there be on whether there is an external reality? Would you be willing to bet your life that you have a life? There is no sense here. Here there is just believing or not believing. There are no degrees.

Daniel   I agree that it's hard to make sense of a betting scenario involving the proposition that there is an external reality. But that might be thought to be a problem even for saying that there is a distinction here between believing and not believing that there is an external reality. We seem to be allowing that distinction to operate in purely phenomenological terms, without appealing to betting or risk behavior. Then why not allow the distinction between certainty and uncertainty in the same terms?

Lev But what is the phenomenology, Daniel? How does that work? Let us indeed appeal to the phenomenology. If I can believe something without being certain of it then, though I feel that I believe it, I also feel that it would be possible to get me not to believe it. Perhaps even I am vacillating between believing and not believing. But if believing something is necessary, as is believing in an external reality, then there can be no relevant vacillation and no relevant possibility of giving up the belief. If my believing something is necessary then the belief is unshakable, and that means that I am certain. I am certain in the only sense that can apply to this belief.

Daniel I see. Yes. But I'm not entirely convinced, Lev. Vatol may not be able to give up this belief, and at least in that sense there can't be vacillation, but he may still find himself wanting to say, "Maybe this belief is false; maybe there is really no external reality." You need to be able to show that the impossibility-of-doubt thesis implies that Vatol cannot say that. That's not clear to me. It's not clear to me that you have shown this.

Yitzhak Let me make a suggestion about this. I agree with what Lev is saying, though not for exactly the same reasons. I think that in fact it *never* makes sense to talk of belief without certainty, at least if certainty is defined in the way that's relevant to this discussion. I think we should look again at the connections in Williamson between assertion, belief, and certainty. Williamson's position seems to be, as I presented it before, that to assert "*p*, but maybe not-*p*" is contranormative. It violates a norm of assertion. I think something a little different. Of course one can lie when making an assertion. But there is such a thing as a sincere assertion. I think it is *metaphysically impossible* to sincerely assert "*p*, but maybe not-*p*." Williamson talks about *normative* constraints, but I want to talk of *necessary* constraints. Suppose that someone asserts, "Muttel Finkelsten lives in Cleveland, but maybe he doesn't." I think it is not conceivable that this is meant sincerely. Now believing is the subjective counterpart of sincere assertion. If you cannot possibly sincerely assert something, you cannot possibly believe it. A helpful picture is of someone who thinks out loud. We can listen to what he is thinking. Suppose that someone is thinking out loud and we hear him saying, "Let's see. Where is Muttel these days? Oh, yes, he is living in Cleveland, though he may not be living there." I think we can make no sense of this. That is not a possible belief that we have heard being vocalized. Believing something is incompatible with thinking that it may not be so. Now I don't think that for our purposes we need to concern ourselves with how the expression "certain that *p*" is used. The crucial point is that the impossibility-of-doubt thesis entails that it is impossible for Vatol to think, "Maybe it's all a hallucination." And that is the only thought that could allow him to explain in plain language what he is anxious about.

Lev   Why did you say we do not need to concern ourselves with certainty? Knowing how tricky and devious you are, I fathom that there must be something intriguing behind that.

Yitzhak   Well, there are all kinds of familiar problems that Bayesians face in trying to assign probability of 1 to propositions, 1 being the highest degree of probability. Suppose I am certain of p, so that gets a 1, and certain of q, so that gets a 1. Shouldn't I be more certain of their disjunction? So what probability does the disjunction get? It seems that there may somehow be degrees of certainty—I think this may actually have been implied by Austin.[32] But I don't think we need to deal with that problem for our purposes. We might hold that Vatol is less certain that there is an external world than that each thing is identical with itself. That wouldn't matter for our issue. All that matters is that, since Vatol sincerely asserts, perhaps only to himself, "There is an external reality," he can't possibly also sincerely assert, "but maybe there isn't." It's not possible to believe, "There is an external reality, but maybe there isn't." And since, according to the impossibility-of-doubt view, he can't say, "Maybe there isn't," he can't explain what he is anxious about. That's how the argument ought to work, for Lev.

Lev   Perhaps it works like this, Yitzhak. There are degrees of certainty and Bayesians must shout the number one at higher and higher decibel levels. Then Jewish Bayesians will hire cantors to be with them. I have a cousin in France who is a cantor and struggling, so I am happy with this idea.

Yitzhak   I once asked a Bayesian philosopher if he really wanted to say that his degree of belief in the existence of his children is less than one. He said, "You'd have to know my kids." Yeah. Important to have all the relevant data.

Daniel   Okay. Good, good. Your formulation sounds very interesting, Yitz. Belief entails certainty at least in the crucial sense of precluding "Maybe it isn't so." I'll have to think more about it, but it initially sounds right to me. What do you think, Lev?

Lev   As you realize, English is not my first language. It is not even my second language, which is Hebrew. So as I listen to Yitzhak I translate in my mind to Hebrew, *lashon hakodesh*, the sacred language. Now, the Rashba states that Hebrew is also "ikar ha-lashon," which means the intrinsic, essential language.[33] Translating Yitzhak's remarks into *ikar ha-lashon* I find his arguments to be beautiful and to resonate with the angels who guard the portals of truth.

Yitzhak   In short, it does not resonate with you. You know Daniel was raised on Yiddish by his crazed Rumanian *bubbi*, and his head is still on pretty straight. So I think there is still hope for you, Lev.

Lev   Yitzhak, I discover oddly that your latest remarks are not translatable into Hebrew. But let me say, if I might, that I am troubled by one point. You persuade me, Yitzhak, that it is impossible to sincerely assert, "It is the case that *p*, but it may not be the case that *p*." And someone who thinks out loud, in your very beautiful image, cannot be thinking, "It is the case that *p*, but it may not be the case that *p*." It appears that there is such a thing as asserting to oneself, asserting in one's mind, and this asserting in one's mind does seem to be belief, in one understanding of what belief is. But is that the only understanding? That is what troubles me. For I am of the thought— in the Hebrew or French translation this would definitely be so— that it is good to assert, "Cohen allows that Muttel may have moved, but he *believes* that Muttel is still in Cleveland." Here it seems that what Cohen believes is something that he would not be willing to assert.

Yitzhak   I notice that you placed a stress on the word "believes" in your report of Cohen's alleged belief.

Daniel   So what, Yitz? I think that Lev's point is valid. If, according to you, it is impossible for Cohen to believe that, although Muttel may not live in Cleveland, he does live in Cleveland, placing a stress on "belief" shouldn't change this. I think that Lev's example shows that the expression "believes that *p*" is semantically ambiguous. It may express *outright belief* that *p*, where outright belief is indeed constituted by one's being prepared to sincerely assert *p*, perhaps in one's mind, as Lev put it. But it may also express *belief to a high degree*, where I suppose a context of some sort would determine what qualifies as high enough. In the latter sense of "belief," believing is not connected to assertion, neither necessarily nor normatively. Jonathan Adler, who elaborates the connection between belief and assertion, worries about the obvious fact that one often says, and without violating any norms, things of the form, "I believe that *p*, though I admit it may be that not-*p*." And, if I understand him correctly, Adler makes the heroic suggestion that when someone utters, "I believe that *p*," he expresses the fact that he does *not* believe that *p*, that he only believes that *p* is probable, that is, he only believes *p* to a degree, but doesn't believe it *simpliciter*, since to believe *simpliciter* is to believe outright.[34] That seems untenable to me. Certainly if I say, "I believe that Muttel is in Cincinatti," I am expressing something that you could rightly express by saying,

"Daniel believes that Muttel is in Cincinatti." There is not some special enforced first-person idiom involved here. What there is, rather, is good old semantic ambiguity, two senses of "believes." We can see the ambiguity further in this example: "Although Cohen allows that Muttel may no longer be in Cleveland, I believe that Muttel is still living there." In this case it's clear that the first-person expression "I believe that" is being used to express an outright belief.

Yitzhak   Yeah. Maybe you're right that there is semantic ambiguity here, but of a peculiar sort, I think. It seems that the primary sense of "believes" is outright belief. That's the default interpretation. There normally has to be some special form of pragmatic indicator to push one towards the alternative interpretation. In Lev's example the stress indicates that something is up, and even without the stress, since we're told that Cohen allows that Muttel may no longer be there, his belief that Muttel is there can't coherently be an outright belief. But if we're just told, "Cohen believes that Muttel lives there," we'll take that to mean an outright belief, I think. The first-person case is special, as Adler says—because if someone says, "I believe that p," why didn't he just say, "p"? The extra words clue us into something's being up, and then we retreat to the other interpretation, the one in which it's not an outright belief.

Lev   The extra words induce a *diyuk*. We ask, "la-afukei mai," and the answer is *la-afukei* outright belief.*

---

* A *diyuk* is a Talmudic inference, often from the appearance of superfluous words in a received text. The superfluous words invite the question, "La-afukei mai?" that is, "to exclude what?"

Yitzhak Exactly.

Daniel Good. Excellent. I think that sums up where we now stand. Let me say that I am not convinced that "believes" in the strong outright sense deserves to be called the "primary" sense, as Yitzhak has just stated, but I don't think we need to settle that.[35] We are taking the impossibility-of-doubt view to preclude doubt in the sense of requiring a cognitive state in which one is prepared to sincerely assert, "There is an external reality." That cognitive state is what we call "outright belief." For the purposes of our discussion let us simply call it "belief," ignoring for our purposes an apparently different sense of "belief." This required cognitive state of belief is incompatible with a different cognitive state in which one is prepared to sincerely assert, "It may be that there is no external reality." This second cognitive state is what we are calling "doubt," and is ruled out by the impossibility-of-doubt thesis. This is the thesis Lev will defend.

Yitzhak Right. I think that is where we now stand. But there is one further point. I'm inclined to agree with those who've said that believing *simpliciter*, that is, outright, may easily fluctuate back and forth with believing to a degree. This can happen with the blink of an eye, because of a change of conversational context or maybe even because of a change in a person's mood.[36] We agreed to keep the context fixed to one in which we are engaged in the Cartesian reflection, so I suppose we don't have to concern ourselves with a change of context, but maybe the fluctuation can occur without a change of context. Does that affect our discussion?

Lev   I too am inclined to agree with that view of easy fluctuations between belief outright that *p*, which excludes the doubting judgment, "It may be that not *p*," and degree of belief that does not exclude some doubt. But I hold that a fixed Archimedean point is belief in external reality. That belief must always be outright.

Yitzhak   Because of an argument you're eventually going to give us?

Lev   In my argument I will hold that one's existence must necessarily include certain special feelings directed to external reality, and these feelings cannot possibly be accompanied by the doubting thought, "Maybe there is no such reality." For example, it is necessary that I have certain feelings of self-esteem, and these feeling must be directed to how I am relating to other beings. Such feelings therefore cannot go together with the thought, "Maybe there are no other beings."

Daniel   Ah . . . Hmm . . . Interesting.

Yitzhak   Russell reports somewhere about some mathematician who said of Christianity, "Interesting if true."

Daniel   Lev will give us his argument later. Good, good. I surmise that for the purposes of the argument Lev will give it does not really matter whether we talk of "believing," or "being certain," or "being sure." What will be crucial, apparently, is that the doubting judgment "It may not be so" is excluded.[37] So we will continue to use "believes" in a sense that excludes that judgment . . . Good, good.

Further connections between "doubt," "anxiety," and "knowledge"

Lev   And may I add an observation?

Daniel   Of course. Please.

Lev   In the example of Vatol what is most clear is the fact about his anxiety. It is that fact that guides us in understanding facts about his knowledge, belief, certainty, doubt.

Yitzhak   The anxiety-first doctrine!

Lev   What is most clear is that insofar as Vatol is a rational human being he *must* feel anxious. And he must feel anxious just *because* he is a rational human being. I hope that even a philosopher like Williamson will agree eventually with this. Now anxiety is most often directed outwards, not inwards. A man may be anxious about his child's health. His wife may then become anxious that his anxiety will lead to his having a heart attack. He too may have this second anxiety. The first anxiety is directed outward, to his daughter's health, the second is directed inwards. It is clear that Vatol's anxiety is directed outward, directed indeed to the existence of what is external to him. He cannot well describe the object, the target, of his anxiety except by asserting that maybe there is no external reality. But this he cannot do. The impossibility-of-doubt view says that he can only sincerely assert, to others or to himself, "There is an external reality." It is therefore impossible for him to sincerely assert, to others or to himself, "It may be that there is no external reality." That is the central point.

Yitzhak I agree that the Vatol example should be our intuitive touchstone in this discussion. But let me take the stress off of this "anxiety" business for a minute. It seems clear, at least to the three of us, that Vatol has, all things considered, reason to doubt, that is, reason not to believe. This seems to indicate at least one good sense of the words "reason, all things considered, not to believe, but to doubt." That provides us with the sense of "reason," the sense of "believes," and the sense of "doubt" that concerns us in this discussion. And a major question for us is whether we, who do not live in a world filled with vat-people, have in this sense reason to doubt, reason not to believe.

Daniel Yes. That's very good. But I also think that Lev is pointing out an assumption that we have been making in this discussion about a connection between anxiety and doubts of external reality. This already came out earlier in your remark, Yitzhak, that if you doubted external reality, you would be terrified out of your mind. My point is that you apparently were not at all attracted to the option of saying something like, "It may be that there is in fact no external reality, but that is so improbable that it need not concern me." You seemed to take it for granted that if you doubted external reality, that is, if your thought is, "Maybe there is no external reality," so that you suspended your outright belief in external reality, then no addendum about probabilities would save you from anxiety.

Lev Such seemed to be the attitude conveyed by Descartes early in the Meditations. If belief of external reality is suspended, then whatever one judges about probabilities, one must be in a state of extreme mental distress. Such also seemed to be Hume's attitude.

Daniel Yes. Perhaps. That is, in any case, an assumption we are making. Perhaps it amounts to this: If the possibility that there is no external world seems so remote that even reflecting on it does not give one reason to feel anxious, then one has no reason to withhold asserting the proposition that there is an external world. One should then believe outright that there is an external world, even if perhaps at less than the highest decibel level of certainty.

Yitzhak So let me be clear about this. You're saying that our assumption is that, when one reflects on the matter, one has reason to doubt external reality in the relevant sense if, and only if, one has reason to feel anxious about whether there is an external reality. I do personally find that quite compelling, though I wouldn't necessarily expect everyone else to make that connection between doubt and anxiety. But I suppose the connection clarifies further what at least the three of us mean in this context by "doubt."

Daniel But let me ask you one further thing, Yitz, though it may not be directly relevant to the course of our discussion. You suggested that Williamson's norm connecting belief to assertion ought to be changed to a necessity. Now Williamson also has a more famous norm connecting both assertion and belief to knowledge. It says, "You should not assert p if you don't know p."[38] That obviously can't be converted into a necessity, since it's certainly possible to make a mistake and assert something you don't know.

Yitzhak Yeah. Right, right. But there's another spin on this. Berislav Marušić argues for what I think is an improvement on Williamson's norm.[39] Marušić proposes this: "You should not assert p if you don't

believe that you know *p*." Now that could be converted into the
necessity, "It's impossible to sincerely assert *p* if you don't believe you
know *p*."

Daniel   So is that what you think?

Yitzhak   I'm not sure what to say about it. Religious faith, very
dramatically in someone like Kierkegaard, often seems to involve the
stance, "Certainly God exists, I have no doubt of this, but I don't
know it." I don't think that has to be insincere. Maybe it comes out
better if it's put: "Certainly God exists, I have no doubt of this, but I
don't have *knowledge* of this," changing "know" to "knowledge" and
placing a stress on it. Lev mentioned earlier that Moore attributed a
stance of that sort to Russell and other professed skeptics. Moore
claimed that what Russell really meant to say was something like,
"Certainly there is an external world, I have no doubt of this, but I
don't have *knowledge* of this." I think it's fairly clear that in Stroud's
The Significance of Philosophical Scepticism he often has the stance,
"Certainly there is an external world, I have no doubt of this, but it
may be that I do not have *knowledge* of this."[40] I'm not sure if I want
to say that these stances are unintelligible or even contra-normative.
By the way, Marušić holds that there are central examples where his
norm does not operate. So this is a tangled matter, and I think we
don't have to get involved in it. Let me add that, despite these
complications, one important point to take away is that, with the
possible exception of certain special cases, the following principle
holds: One cannot have an epistemic reason to believe something
unless one has an epistemic reason to believe that one knows it. I
think this helps to give us a sense of what we are demanding of

ourselves, and of Vatol, in the way of having a reason to believe in external reality: there must be a reason to believe that we know there is an external reality.

Daniel Okay, good. Good. I think we've cleared up some of the preliminaries. Then let's go on.

Yitzhak We must go on. We can't go on. We must go on. *Veiter*! [Onward!]

Interlude: Waiting for Godot

Daniel "We can't go on. We must go on." *Waiting for Godot*?[41]

Lev Yitzhak! Yitzhak! I understand why unconsciously you said that. *Waiting for Godot*. There is more epistemological truth in that play than in a hundred typical works of analytic philosophy.

Yitzhak That's utterly insane, of course.

Lev Two men, they are weird and comical looking characters, they wander about on some empty road. They are lost and abandoned ... Lost and abandoned ... And they wait ... They wait for this Godot to come. We do not know why. Yes? It seems they do not know either, why they wait. Now it happens at the end of Act I—*Ich mein*—a messenger from this Godot—a child, a young boy—comes there on the road to tell them that, this time again, Godot has been detained; he will not be coming that day. One of the men says to the boy he should tell Godot that he has seen them. And then this man says to

that child, "You have seen us, haven't you?" This question for a
philosopher will resonate in a special way. "You have seen us, haven't
you?" It is like trying to check whether you are dreaming by asking
the person next to you. That could not be meant seriously. But, in the
play, the question—"You have seen us, haven't you?"—somehow *is*
meant seriously, even though it is obvious nonsense. Yes?

A special kind of epistemic anxiety emanates from the characters
in Samuel Beckett's play, a distinctive sense of epistemic
bewilderment, a sense of being at bottom lost, of being engulfed in a
kind of transcendental fog, a fog that cannot possibly lift. Yes? I am
calling it transcendental because the feeling, the feeling generated,
the feeling generated in Beckett's play is that this epistemic fog . . . *Ich
mein* . . . this epistemic fog that engulfs these characters, the fog that
engulfs these characters, it, this fog, is not a matter of contingent
human psychology. It is rather, I should say, transcendental in the
sense that it is a necessary condition of any reflective consciousness
. . . *Ich mein* . . . any consciousness, any consciousness capable of
reflecting on and evaluating its situation. This is the feeling, the
atmosphere, in Samuel Beckett's play. And with this transcendental
fog, this transcendental bewilderment, there must of course go with
it a special kind of anxiety. Anxiety about *what*? Anxiety about *what*?
Samuel Beckett's play answers this question poetically, perhaps
mystically. The only answer. That is the only answer.

Yitzhak   The fog that will not lift; The sun that will not shine; The
earth that will not give its gift; To Muttel Finkelstein.

Daniel   What? What on earth is that? "Shine" does not rhyme with
"Finkelstein."

Yitzhak This bothers you a lot?

Daniel Where on earth did you get that ditty from?

Yitzhak It just popped into my mind. Whole. Unbidden, but frankly, not entirely unwelcome.

Daniel Okay . . . Okay, Lev, please go on. Please go on.

Lev Yes. Yes. The fog. Yes, Yitzhak. Vatol . . . Vatol has a wife. Let us imagine this. They are very close. He shares everything with her. He gets off the phone with his brother. What can he say to her?

Yitzhak We'll always have Paris, shweetheart—maybe.

Daniel Come on, Yitz!

Lev What can he say to her? The truth of his anxiety presses in upon him. His brother's voice, his brother's illusions, are too fresh in his mind. He will be careless and inattentive on another day. But not this day. Not yet. The issue is too *salient*. As it is for us on those occasions when we deeply immerse ourselves in the Cartesian reflection. Of course doubt is impossible. He cannot possibly doubt the reality of his life, he cannot possibly doubt what he has done, who he is. Can he speak to her? But he must speak to her. He must speak to her. He will say: You have seen me, haven't you? You have seen me, haven't you?

Daniel Ah . . . Ah . . . Good . . . Good, good. You have made it very clear, Lev, why this play means so much to you . . . What's the matter, Yitzhak?

Yitzhak   Nothing.

Lev   You are feeling well, Yitzhak?

Yitzhak   I'm fine. I'm fine ... Before we go further I need to ask you something, Lev.

Lev   What is it, Yitzhak?

Yitzhak   Let me get something straight before we move on, Lev. You're saying that we ought to take seriously the possibility that our whole lives are just long hallucinations? Is that right? Are you completely out of your mind? I mean this. Are you *mamash* [literally] a crazy man? You are saying that I should take seriously the possibility that it's all a hallucination? Are you actually saying that? I'm not joking! Are you literally crazy?

Lev   I am saying that you are necessarily closed off from doubting that there is an external world. Am I then saying that you should take this possibility seriously? You would have to be explaining to me what you mean by "taking it seriously." *Ich mein*, did Descartes take it seriously? Did Hume? Did Peter Unger? Does Barry Stroud? You would have to be explaining to me what you mean by "taking it seriously."

Yitzhak   But you want me to be anxious the way Vatol is.

Lev   Yitzhak. I want you to be happy. That is what I want for you. I have not requested to be cast in the role of a demented witch doctor prescribing anxiety to a reluctant tribe.

Yitzhak   Then what do you want? What do you want?

Daniel   Listen! Listen! *Her zich ein. Kinder.* I think we are drifting off the track a little. Let's continue to discuss the specific philosophical points Lev seems to be advancing. Psychological assessments aren't necessary. Okay?

Yitzhak   Yeah. Yeah. That's right. That's right. Let's keep going.

A connection to Nagel's skepticism

Daniel   Okay. Good ... Then let's move on. Lev, you mentioned Nagel before. And last week you had mentioned Nagel and Feyerabend. I begin to see the connection to Nagel. I remember his paper "The Absurd," and I can see that it has some affinities to what you are trying to get at.

Yitzhak   What I remember from that paper is that Nagel disparages Camus' ideas about absurdity as being a bit self-pitying. Camus, who fought against the Nazis in the French resistance is too self-pitying for Nagel, who does admittedly risk his life frequently by flying to his apartment in Paris.

Daniel   That remark is completely ridiculous, Yitzhak, as well as offensive!

Yitzhak   Yeah, I know. But I operate on the principle of dialectical fairness that you can go after philosophers who make a lot more money than you make.

Daniel   What is this, *kinas sofrim*? Or *kinas ashirim*?*

Yitzhak   Right.

Daniel   But you admire Nagel, Lev?

Lev   I admire him very deeply. I believe that Thomas Nagel understands how meaningful the issue of skepticism is, how meaningful it is to our lives. In this he seems to be unique among recent philosophers, of course with the exception of Wittgenstein.

Yitzhak   Tell me something, Lev, why do you say Wittgenstein is an exception? Where do you see in Wittgenstein anything about how meaningful skepticism is to our lives?

Lev   Where do we see this in Wittgenstein? Where do we not see it? Wittgenstein's understanding of the existential depth and meaning of the issue of skepticism is apparent in every word of "On Certainty."[42]

Yitzhak   Right. Right. Every word in Wittgenstein is dripping, *dripping* with honesty and anguish. With honest anguish. With anguished honesty. Yeah . . . But, wait a minute, Lev, what about Moore? Even Wittgenstein reportedly considered Moore's defense of common sense to be significant.

Lev   I believe Wittgenstein at that point mistook Moore's simple-mindedness for honesty.

---

* *Kinas sofrim* is envy of scholars, the one form of competitive envy approved by the Rabbis. *Kinas ashirim* is envy of the rich.

Yitzhak You think G.E. Moore was not honest? He was renowned for his honesty.

Lev I do not believe it is possible to be both honest and as shallow as Moore.

Daniel You're talking about emotional shallowness, not intellectual shallowness.

Lev I do not believe there is really a distinction.

Yitzhak You're *mamash* a complete idiot! You have heard me, haven't you?

Daniel Take it easy, Yitzhak . . .

Lev No, Yitzhak. Listen. Yitzhak. I did not intend to belittle Moore.

Yitzhak You did not intend to belittle Moore? I think you need to check the word "belittle" in the OED.

Daniel Look! We're not talking about Moore, are we? We were talking about Nagel. Please! Let's get back to that . . . So you agree with what Nagel says in "The Absurd," Lev?

Lev I believe it is a wonderful paper. I agree with many things in it. But I believe that at the end Thomas Nagel does not delve deeply enough into the phenomenology of skeptical reflection.

Daniel The phenomenology of skeptical reflection. Is that our topic, Lev?

Lev I believe that is part of our topic. Yes, Daniel.

Daniel   Okay, please go on.

Lev   Thomas Nagel states in "The Absurd" that skepticism about external reality cannot be refuted. I am sure he means by this to imply that we have reason to doubt. He states that reason cannot save us from this doubt. We are saved by something deeper in us that makes it impossible for us to doubt. I am—how do the British philosophers say it?—I am on board, I am on board with this, although I will want to explain more later about what this deeper thing in us is that makes it impossible to doubt.

Daniel   You'll talk about that when you give your explanation of the impossibility-of-doubt view.

Lev   Yes, yes. I want now to comment on what Thomas Nagel says in "The Absurd" is the effect on us, the effect on our feelings and attitudes, when we realize that reason cannot save us from this doubt. The effect, he says, is irony. We confront our lives with ironic resignation. I am of the opinion that in saying this Thomas Nagel keeps himself at a distance from the true phenomenology of skeptical reflection. What is this irony? *Eich nafelu gibborim*: How the mighty are fallen.[43] That is the essential meaning of the ironic resignation Thomas Nagel alludes to. It is, as Thomas Nagel explains, essentially to acknowledge our pretensions, our pretense of being more than we actually are. We acknowledge the false pretension of reason to rule our lives when we realize that reason cannot save us from doubt that there is an external reality. So there is irony. With all of this I agree. There is irony. We are indeed brought low from our pedestal. But that cannot be all. Vatol must indeed live his life with the ironic recognition that his reason cannot save him from doubting, cannot save him from the thought that what he attributes to his brother is really applicable to he himself. But there must also be something seething beneath the irony. For the most part this will not be consciously felt. For the most part Vatol will live with carelessness and inattention. And perhaps with an ironic posture. But there must be something seething beneath the posture of irony. And on some occasions Vatol will not be able to avoid feeling this, feeling what is seething below.

Daniel   And that is? Anxiety, bewilderment, a sense of being lost, and abandoned. Is that it? . . .

Yitzhak   Lev thinks that Nagel's irony is a posture, that underneath his N.Y. tough guy's smirk he is terrified. Imagine Bill Murray standing over a table and saying, "This table really exists." Lev wants to wipe the ironic smirk off Nagel's face. He wants to see Nagel on the floor, sobbing, and calling out for Thompson Clarke.

Lev   Yitzhak. There is a scene in *Waiting for Godot*. One of the men says he had a dream. The other says, "Don't tell me!"

Yitzhak   You mean this applies not just to nightmares, but also to garish fantasies and daydreams.

Lev   I believe it might. But there is much vagueness in the norm. Perhaps I precisify. Which may itself be contra-normative.

Yitzhak   Or impolitic. I think premature precisification is the main cause of divorce. And also the reason why the *Lubabitcher rebbe* has not returned from the dead.

Lev   Do not tell me!

Daniel   So I am trying to understand this better, Lev. You think that Nagel makes a mistake of some sort?

Lev   I believe, Daniel, that Thomas Nagel does not go deeply enough.

Yitzhak   Let me try to get one thing straight here. You think, Lev, that when Nagel says that skepticism can't be refuted by reason, he implies that our situation is just like Vatol's?

Lev   No, not just like Vatol's. Carelessness and inattention is much easier for us than for him. But on those occasions when we are not careless and inattentive, on those occasions when we seriously engage in reflection, what difference, Yitzhak, do you think Nagel could have between us and Vatol?

Yitzhak   I don't know. Maybe some probability difference.

Lev   Yes? Perhaps Vatol considers there to be a probability of .5 that his life is a long hallucination and we consider the probability to be only .3. And that difference of probabilities is the difference between our irony and what Vatol must feel.

Daniel   Didn't we agree earlier that if one has reason to doubt then one has reason to be anxious?

Yitzhak   Look, I don't really know what's going on here. Both Nagel and Lev are wrong in thinking that we have reason to doubt.

Daniel   Okay, that is a different issue. But I want Lev now to explain more where he thinks Nagel goes wrong.

Lev I believe that Thomas Nagel avoids discussing those feelings and attitudes that cannot be explained in plain terms. If I am Vatol and you ask me why I feel irony, if you ask me what I am being ironic *about*, I can answer this in plain terms. My beliefs, my most essential beliefs, are not as great, as powerful as I had pretended. Thomas Nagel gives an analogy. A man takes back a wayward wife. The man thereafter views his marriage with ironic resignation. It is not the vaunted marriage he expected. It is the same for my beliefs. My irony about my beliefs is given a plain and straightforward explanation. But when you ask me as Vatol what I am *anxious about* I have no answer. I say that my beliefs are ultimately groundless. You say, "*So?*" I say, the ground has been knocked out from under me. You say, "*So?*" I say, so, maybe, maybe ... You say, "Maybe *what?*" There is no meaningful way for me ending the sentence. For I cannot sincerely say, "Maybe it is just a long hallucination."

Daniel So Nagel does not acknowledge the anxiety that must lie beneath the irony because there would not be any way to explain that anxiety in plain language.

Lev In one place Samuel Beckett says, "There is nothing to express, nothing with which to express, nothing from which to express, no power to express, no desire to express, together with the obligation to express."[44]

Yitzhak Lev, you actually memorized that whole thing from Beckett? Wow, what dedication, what *mesirus nefesh* [dedication of the soul]. Express, express, express. I have a good mnemonic for it. Five. You know, the number 5 train. Express to the Bronx ... But are we really asking this question about Nagel? No, wait! I take that back. That's not an idiom I want to use in front of Lev. I meant to say that this question we're talking about seems exceedingly weird to me. We're asking whether Nagel ought to be ironic or anxious? Should he be smirking or quaking all the way to the bank? Is that it? That's our question? What is this, philosophy or some sort of soap opera for lunatics?

Daniel   I'm sorry, Yitzhak, I don't get what your problem is. One of our most eminent living philosophers, Tom Nagel, has a famous paper in which he says that skepticism can't be refuted and that therefore a certain attitude, an attitude of ironic resignation, is the appropriate existential stance. Why should we not be having a discussion about that claim? I think the underlying question is what it can mean to be *serious* when philosophizing about skepticism. It's the question Lev asked you earlier. What can it mean to take skepticism seriously? I think that Stroud has at times probably agreed with Nagel that skepticism can't be refuted, and I think that he, like Nagel, has taken that to imply that we have reason to doubt. The existential implication of this for Stroud, as far as I can tell, is to write more philosophy papers. I don't think that's what it can mean to take skepticism seriously. Nagel seems to dig deeper. But Lev is arguing that he doesn't dig deep enough. Irony can't be the full response to taking skepticism seriously. You seem to be missing the main point, Yitz. The question is not, "Should it be irony or anxiety?" Lev is saying that there has to be both. But, whereas the irony is directed towards a truth that can be articulated in plain terms, the underlying anxiety is directed towards a truth that we are somehow debarred from articulating. That's the main point.

Interlude: philosophy and comedy

Yitzhak   Hey, what is all this agreement between you two guys? This is beginning to sound like one of those Socratic dialogues. "Will you agree, Shmuckius, that suchandsuch?"—"Of course, Socrates."

Daniel   Listen, Yitzhak, it's not a matter of agreement or disagreement. It's a matter of not allowing you to dictate what it's permissible to discuss. I don't see any reason to worry that Nagel's idea about skepticism and irony is an improper subject for philosophical discussion.

Yitzhak   What worries me, actually, is that no one really takes this stuff seriously except for Lev.

Lev   Why does that worry you, Yitzhak?

Yitzhak   I'm worried about your publication enterprise. Irony sells a lot better than anxiety.

Daniel   What would be a journal that might welcome a highly unorthodox approach like Lev's?

Yitzhak   The Phil Review!

Daniel   Yitzhak is always a comedian, Lev, among his other virtues.

Lev   Yitzhak has indeed many virtues. Humor can be most honest. We understand that Samuel Beckett was a comedic genius. *Waiting for Godot* he called a tragicomedy. In Beckett it was as in the Hindu myth of turtles on turtles all the way down. The jokes in Beckett cascade down upon each other without limit. But a truth shines out from the comedy. In Beckett the truth is not concealed. In Beckett's comedy the truth is there for all to see.

Yitzhak   Is the truth inside the comedy or is the comedy inside the truth? But maybe that's the same modulo a topological homeomorphism.

Daniel   That's not a homeomorphism. Is it?

Yitzhak   Did you guys hear this one? You run into an old acquaintance you haven't seen for a long time. You say, "How're you doing? How is everything? How are your folks?" The guy says, "They died." You say, "Oh, I'm very sorry to hear that. I always enjoyed seeing them. Well, how is your lovely wife doing? Please say hello from me." The guy says, "She died too." You say, "No! How terrible! I am so, so sorry. How are your kids taking all of this?" The guy says, "You're gonna laugh. But they died too."

Daniel   That's it? That's the end? That's supposed to be funny, Yitz? . . . Lev, you're actually laughing at this?

Lev   I mean . . . *Ich mein* . . . *Ich mein* . . . It is a Wittgenstein joke on the grammar of "your're gonna laugh."

Yitzhak   You're gonna laugh. But the whole thing may just be a long hallucination.

Daniel   Ah . . . I see . . .

Yitzhak   Whistling in the dark is permitted as long as one doesn't pretend that it's not dark.

Daniel   Okay.

Yitzhak Laughter in the cemetery is unseemly, but nervous giggling is permitted.

Daniel Okay, Yitzhak. Okay.

Lev Is that from a Midrash?

Yitzhak I hope not.

Lev In this connection we might also discuss Paul Feyerabend's Dadaism in the philosophy of science.[45] Pascal said that to mock philosophy is to philosophize truly.[46] Professor Feyerabend was aspiring to reveal the true nature of science by mocking science.

Yitzhak Yeah, Feyerabend was always good for a laugh at Berkeley. And I recall that a number of female students were saying to him, "You're my Dadaist."

Daniel *Kinas sofrim* again?

Yitzhak Yeah.

Daniel Listen, Lev, I don't think we'll have time to discuss Feyerabend today. Can you tell us now your explanation for why doubt is impossible?

A challenge to Lev's assumptions about epistemic anxiety

Yitzhak I want to say something. I said before that I thought if I doubted external reality I would be terrified out of my mind. But I'm not claiming that everyone else has to feel that way about it. How do I know what other people might feel? Apparently some ancient Greek skeptics said that doubting everything induces a certain mood of tranquility, of peacefulness.[47] Therefore, Vatol would need fewer back rubs.

Lev   The ancient Greeks! In "The Apology" Socrates is depicted as going to his death in the manner of a man departing his home in the morning and wondering whether he will find a seat on the trolley.

Yitzhak   "Let's see. What's on my schedule for today? Oh, yes, dying."

Lev   If we were to read Sartre's "The Wall" in juxtaposition with "The Apology," we could feel that we are literally addressing two different species. One human. Of course, it is not a difference of species but a difference between a measure of honesty and the total lack of it.

Yitzhak   You know how in these old live T.V. shows there is a guy up there with signs for the audience saying, "Laugh," "Applaud," and so on. The next time *Waiting for Godot* is in town you should get a job standing on the stage with signs like, "Tremble," "Squirm." "Howl." You're apparently the one person who knows the right reaction to everything.

Daniel   But death is not our topic.

Lev   That is correct.

Yitzhak   I heard a colleague give a talk once in which he said that skepticism about external reality induces in him a feeling of exhilarated rootlessness.[48] I guess like a wandering Jew wandering from one possible world to another. That's not your reaction, and it's certainly not mine. But couldn't someone react that way?

Lev   Yes, Yitzhak, I will tell you how. You recall some of those Berkeley radicals with us in graduate school, I reflect on those particular ones who were exhilarated to throw off the yoke of normal life demands, as they were going home on breaks having their mothers do their laundry. So it is with the tranquil or exhilarated "skeptic." If the background of normal life remains fixed, *Ich mein*, fixed in the background of consciousness, but is being deliberately kept out of view, one can feel tranquility or exhilaration, *Ich mein*, by the fantasy, the make-believe, of skepticism. Against that fixed background one may be enjoying the fantasy of eliminating that background. But the background cannot possibly be eliminated! The fantasy of tranquility or exhilaration in skepticism about external reality is a grotesque fraud. If the Cartesian reflection may in some manner, *Ich mein*, in some sense, be a challenge or an undermining to that necessarily fixed background, the abyss, yes, the abyss that becomes partly visible is at the opposite end of the universe of such attitudes as tranquility or exhilaration. Those who do not understand even that much, understand nothing whatever in the topic of skepticism.

Yitzhak   So you say.

Daniel   Okay. Good. Then let's hear your defense of the claim that doubt is impossible, Lev.

Yitzhak   Can I request that we change the order of this discussion? Really, the most central question is whether we, given our experiences, do have reason to doubt. Certainly many philosophers during the last century have denied this. I think many would say that Vatol has reason to doubt because his experience gives him reason to doubt, whereas our experience does not give us reason to doubt.

Daniel So you would prefer to discuss that issue before turning to Lev's account of the impossibility-of-doubt view?

Yitzhak Yeah. Let's cut to the chase. Get to the punch line. Get to the main dish. To the main course.

Lev I detect that Yitzhak is a bit hungry.

Yitzhak That's true. I am. Baloney, baloney, everywhere, but not a drop to eat.

Daniel We'll go out and get something after we finish this ... So, what do you say, Lev? Are you prepared to give an argument that we have reason to doubt in our actual situation?

Lev *Hineni**

Daniel Good.

Yitzhak *Hineni.* "Here I am." That was Avraham's response when God called on him to go out and sacrifice his son Yitzhak.

Lev However, you must try to recall the happy outcome to that adventure, Yitzhak.

Yitzhak Right.

Daniel So go ahead, Lev.

---

* Literally, "here I am," conveying that one is ready for a task.

Act II

Vatol and Us

Lev I first want to be exacting from the two of you a promise. You have agreed that Vatol has reason to doubt. He has reason to give up, to suspend, his normal beliefs about external reality. I am now arguing that our situation is in this regard the same as Vatol's. If he has reason to doubt, then so we do. Now I want you to give me your vow that you will not change your judgment about Vatol. Yes? When the going gets rough, *azoy vee mir zugt* [as one says], you will not salvage yourself by saying that we do indeed have the same reason to doubt that Vatol has, because he too has no reason to doubt, like us.

Daniel You want me to promise that I won't retract my statement that Vatol has reason to doubt? I have no trouble making that promise. I think it's completely clear that Vatol has reason to doubt. I wouldn't expect anyone to deny that.

Yitzhak I agree. I'll commit myself to that. By the way, Lev, how is your garbled English coming along? Are we ever going to get any relief from that?

Lev *Ich mein ...*

Daniel   That is not worth bringing up, Yitzhak! Go on, Lev, continue with what you were saying.

The n-to-n+1 argument

Lev   Now I will ask you this. Imagine that you acquire evidence that makes you to believe that many years ago there were vat-people but they no longer exist. The delicacies do not matter. Let us pretend that this planet has existed for a trillion years. People from another galaxy lived here in the past and created many vat-people. But that civilization and all those many vat-people were destroyed a trillion years ago. Would that have an effect on your epistemic situation? If you have no reason to doubt now, would that discovery give you reason to doubt?

Daniel   I may be starting to see what trap is being set up here, but I'll just answer intuitively. It doesn't seem that those events that happened a trillion years ago would have any effect at all on whether I have reason to doubt. What do you say, Yitz?

Yitzhak   Yeah. I'll go along with that for now. That seems right. And since I think that, as things stand, I have no reason to doubt, it follows that I would have no reason to doubt if I believed that there were vat-people who went out of existence a trillion years ago.

Lev   Now this. I wish that you will consider a series of cases. We start with Vatol, who we can now also call Vatol-sub-zero, and then Vatol-sub-one, and on and on, until we have Vatol-sub-n, for a very

large n that is equal to a trillion years. Yes? Vatol-sub-zero, our
original Vatol, believes that numerous vat-people exist at that time;
Vatol-sub-one believes that numerous vat-people existed up to one
hour ago but they were then destroyed; Vatol-sub-two believes that
numerous vat-people existed up to two hours ago but they were then
destroyed; and on and on. You can see this? In general, Vatol-sub-n
believes that numerous vat-people existed up to n hours ago but
they were then destroyed.

Yitzhak   I smell a sorites argument coming. Where's Williamson
when you need him? Did I ever tell you guys my idea of having in
philosophy a new sentential operator, W? "W (p)" means that p is
true modulo the kinds of counterexamples Williamson will come
up with. So: W (You can't possibly be mistaken about whether you
have a headache). I think that's true. Yeah. But then Williamson will
ask you about W (W (p)), and W (W (W (p))), and W to the nth
power p . . .

Daniel   Ah. Then there's no escape from W.

Lev   But this is not a sorites argument. As you will see. You will,
I am hopeful, not deny the following principle. For any number n,
Vatol-sub-n-plus-one has reason to doubt just the same as
Vatol-sub-n. That one hour can surely make no difference at all to
his having a reason to doubt. Since you say that Vatol has reason
to doubt in the initial case, Vatol-sub-one must have equal reason to
doubt, and then too Vatol-sub-two, and on and on, until we arrive
at Vatol-sub-n, where n is equal to one-trillion-years, who has the
same reason to doubt. Such is contrary to maintaining that you

would have no reason to doubt if you believed there were vat-people many years ago.

Daniel   So why isn't it a sorites argument?

Yitzhak   No, I think he may be right. It's not a sorites argument, if what is meant by a sorites argument is an argument that trades on vagueness, on our inability to draw a precise line in something that varies by degrees under a vague concept. In a sorites argument we begin with the intuition, say, that if someone is tall then his losing (a hundredth of) an inch will still leave him tall. But there is also the intuition that losing an inch will make him *less* tall, tall to a lesser degree. The problem derives from the vagueness of the concept "tall" and our resultant inability to decide where to draw the line between being *less tall* and being *not tall*. This is why the logic of vagueness (supervaluationism or many-valued logics) can be applied to the problem. By contrast, in Lev's n-to-n+1 argument vagueness does not seem to figure at all. There is no initial intuition that if the vat-people went out of existence an hour earlier, there is *less* reason to doubt; on the contrary, the intuition seems to be that there is the *same* degree of reason to doubt. Therefore, we seem to be compelled to go from n to n+1, then to n+2, and so on. If Lev's n to n-plus-one principle is accepted, it does follow that, since Vatol has reason to doubt, so would we if we came to believe that there were numerous vat-people who all went out of existence a trillion years ago.

Daniel   Yitz, I'm not clear about why you say that the initial intuition is that if the vat-people went out of existence an hour earlier, there is the *same* degree of reason to doubt. It seems that in general the fact that something happened longer ago gives one less reason to make inferences about the present. For example, suppose I read authoritative reports that a deadly virus was spreading through the population n hours ago. This might give me a degree of reason to worry that I have the virus. If I read instead that the virus was spreading n+1 hours ago, then I think my reason for worrying is to some very small degree less.

Yitzhak Look, let's be clear about something. The three of us agreed on purely intuitive grounds that Vatol has reason to doubt, that he has reason to distrust all of his perceptual experiences. But we haven't yet tried to give any account of what the nature of this reason is. One thing that is clear is that the reason is not like the one in your example. Even in your example I'm not sure that there is some general rule that there is less reason in the n+1 case than in the n case; I suspect this depends on various background assumptions about the case. But my main point is that your example is essentially different from Vatol's situation. Vatol is not arguing in the normal way from the premise that many vat-people are in the population, so maybe he is a vat-person. We've agreed that at the end of the day Vatol does not have reason to believe that "premise." He winds up with reason to doubt that there are any vat-people; this is because he has reason to doubt everything about external reality, including that there are vat-people. Vatol's argument cannot be, "Since there were vat-people n hours ago, I have reason to doubt that there were vat-people n hours ago." So Vatol's argument is not at all a normal inductive argument from past instances to a present instance like the one in your example. Consider that in your example if you read a further report that an anti-viral vapor was released into the atmosphere and it is no longer possible for anyone to suffer from the virus, this would give you reason to no longer worry. But if Vatol reads a report that some electromagnetic change in the atmosphere has caused the destruction of all the vat-people five minutes ago, and has made it impossible for there to currently be any vat-people, he certainly ought not to be reassured by this that he is not a vat-person. If that could reassure him, he might as well be reassured by the fact that he is walking around the street. Just as he has reason to doubt that he is really walking, he has reason to doubt that he really read any such report. So the logic here is very different from your example. And I'm simply saying that in Vatol's example there seems to be no intuitive difference between the strength of reason in the n case and the n+1 case. At least that's my present intuition. None of this can really be clarified until we get to the bottom of what Vatol's reason to doubt is. I certainly would like to reject the n-to-n+1 principle, but at present I can't see any intuitive way to do that.

Lev   If I may. A difference between the typical sorites argument and the present argument is that in the typical argument we begin with an established fact, for example, that not all people are tall. That fact is not in question. The sorites is then merely a paradox that contradicts the established fact. This is different in the present argument. We do not begin with any established fact. Rather we begin with the intuition that it does not matter to our reason for doubt if vat-people existed many years ago. That is not a settled fact, but merely an initial intuition. But we then find the much *stronger* intuition that it cannot matter to our reason for doubt if the vat-people existed n hours ago or n+1 hours ago. That stronger intuition must then vanquish the weaker one.

Daniel But there must be something wrong with the n-to-n+1 principle. We evidently have a different intuitive reaction to Vatol's epistemic situation than we have to Vatol-sub-trillion's situation. So something must be varying as we go to higher and higher n's.

Lev Yes, yes, Daniel! Something is varying! As you say. Something is varying. There is, yes, a variation in these cases, but not one that is relevant to the question whether there is reason to doubt. It is a variation in the degree of *salience* of the facts about the vat-people.

Daniel Ah. I see, I see. Your idea is that the difference of one hour can make no difference at all to reasons for doubting, but it can make a difference to the salience of those reasons. It's easier to ignore, to forget about people who are long gone than people who are not so long gone. This psychological difference may vary by the hour, or even the minute, at levels that may not be consciously discernible. As regards Hume's advice to try to go about your life by ignoring the skeptical reflections, Vatol-sub-n's situation, for large n's, is far better than Vatol's situation in the initial case. But as regards whether they have reason to doubt, there is no relevant difference between them.

Lev Thank you, Daniel. Let me offer another evidence that we deal here in our initial reaction to examples not with reasons, but with salience of reasons. You both said initially that you would not be bothered if you came to believe that there were vat-people a trillion years ago. But now imagine please that you believed that these vat-people who existed a trillion years ago also had the belief, "There

were vat people who went out of existence a trillion years ago."
This does not worry them because it happened so long before.
Please reflect on that example. Do you not find that you react now
differently? Now you *are* feeling bothered by those vat-people. They
do seem to give you reason to doubt. Why can this be? It cannot be
that their belief about the existence of the long ago vat-people gives
you more reason to doubt. It is rather that this belief that they share
with you makes the reason more salient for you.

Daniel   I think that is a good example, Lev. I think your idea is that
the closer to us the vat-people are the harder it is psychologically to
ignore them, and therefore the more salient seems the reason to
doubt because of them. Closeness may be a matter of temporal
distance, but also a matter of how similar their thoughts are to
us in relevant respects. If they also have the belief, "There were
vat-people who went out of existence a trillion years ago," they
impress themselves more on our attention and the reason to doubt
because of them seems stronger. I suppose that variations of spatial
closeness may also have this effect on us. I agree with you that on
reflection these alterations of closeness don't seem capable of making
a difference to whether there actually is reason to doubt.

Lev   Yes! Yes! Thank you, Daniel. In all of the Vatol examples as
regards whether they have reason to doubt, there is no relevant
difference between them. It is only salience that differs. And the same
is for us. When we *do* attend to the skeptical reflections, there is no
difference between us and Vatol.

Daniel   I think you're moving a bit too quickly, Lev.

Yitzhak Much too quickly. We've committed ourselves to holding that Vatol has reason to doubt. But we're free to change our minds about other things. If your n to n-plus-one principle holds up then we need to retract our previous judgment that finding out about vat-people who existed a trillion years ago would make no epistemic difference. It will make a difference, since I say that we have no reason to doubt as things stand. I'll say that we have no reason to doubt as things stand, even if I admit that we would have reason to doubt in a case in which we found out about the vat-people of a trillion years ago. You're still far from convincing me that, as things stand, we have reason to doubt.

Lev Do you believe, Yitzhak, that in the far future there may be created vat-people? Suppose you believe there is some good chance of this. Does that give you reason to doubt? Or do future vat-people not have the same epistemic effect as past vat-people?

Daniel It's hard to see why the past and future should differ in this way. So this is a good question, Yitz. Do we have to believe that there is no significant probability of future vat-people in order to hold on to the view that we have no reason to doubt?

Yitzhak Right. Yeah. So it seems that the n to n-plus-one principle has to be challenged. We should go back to our initial judgment that it doesn't matter what vat-people existed in the distant past. And the same holds for the distant future.

Daniel But how can you challenge the n to n-plus-one principle? You just said a moment ago that it seems intuitively that an hour difference in when the vat-people existed can't make any difference in how much reason there is to doubt?

A safety condition on belief

Yitzhak   Maybe that isn't so clear. I'm trying to rethink this. I think maybe we should invoke a "safety" condition. In the literature this is generally applied to knowledge.[1] But a kind of internalist safety condition for belief might be this: "You cannot have reason to believe that p if you have reason to believe that it could easily have happened that you would be mistaken in believing that p." In other words, you can't have reason to believe that p if you have reason to believe that there are close worlds at which you believe falsely that p. Now safety is a matter of degree insofar as closeness of worlds is a matter of degree. So the n to n-plus-one principle does generate a typical sorites pattern. For any n, Vatol-sub-n-plus-one is to some degree more safe than Vatol-sub-n. Where exactly to draw the line between what is to be considered safe and what is to be considered not safe is indefinite, but certain cases are definitely on one side of the line and other cases are definitely on the other side of the line. It's definite that in the initial case Vatol is not safe whereas Vatol-sub-n, for very large n's, is safe. So our judgment was correct when we said that it wouldn't matter if we found out that there were vat-people a trillion years ago.

Lev   I do not enjoy this, Yitzhak. Why is Vatol not safe? You are assuming that he could easily have been envatted? Why should you assume this?

Daniel   I think Lev is right, Yitz. We're imagining that only fertilized ova in vitro are made into vat-people. There may be deep laws of biochemistry that necessitate this restriction. Why assume that Vatol could easily have been created in vitro? There may therefore not be any close world in which Vatol is envatted. And he may have no reason to believe there is. But it still seems clear that he has reason to doubt when he gets off the phone with his brother. He has reason to doubt everything about physical reality, including those laws of biochemistry, and including the fact that he was not created in vitro.

Lev More. Suppose this is Vatol Cohen. Was there not discovered a "Cohen gene," a special DNA for *kohanim* who descend through fathers from Aharon, the original priest in the Torah? Suppose this is true. Suppose also that the Cohen gene disqualifies a person from being envatted, again for very deep explanations of biochemistry.

Yitzhak Maybe the brains of *kohanim* are too big to fit into the vat.

Lev Vatol Cohen could not have easily acquired different genes. Perhaps this is even metaphysically impossible for Kripke's "necessity of origins." Then Vatol Cohen is "safe"? Can that matter? I do not think so, Yitzhak. When he finds out about the Cohen gene will he stop feeling anxious? That is senseless.

Daniel I agree. If finding out about the Cohen gene makes him feel that he has no reason to doubt, why is that better than his finding out that he is walking around the street. If he can say, "Ah, what a relief, I've got the Cohen gene, so I can't be envatted," why not simply say, "Ah, what a relief, I'm walking around the street, which I couldn't do if I were a vat-person." His beliefs about whether there is a close world in which he is envatted can't have any effect on his having reason to doubt.

Yitzhak   Well, Vatol Cohen couldn't have spoken to an envatted brother, who would also have the Cohen gene. Unless it's a maternal brother.

Daniel   Obviously it doesn't matter if we change the story so that the guy he speaks to is not his brother. That phone call is just a dramatic device anyway. It's not essential.

Yitzhak   What would be the story about vat-Jews? Could they conform to any *halachah* [Jewish law]? Maybe that's the real issue we should be talking about.

Lev   Yes, a matter of great moment. You should give a speech in *shul* about this, Yitzhak.

Yitzhak   Here is how *nachas* will be in a futuristic world. "Let me introduce you to my clone, the doctor. And if you look into this instrument you can see the brain of my vat-son, the rabbi."

Daniel   So are we prepared to forget about the "safety" condition? If so we seem to be back to accepting the n to n-plus-one principle. And we have to say that finding out about vat-people that existed a trillion years ago would give us reason to doubt. Or even coming to believe that there is some likelihood of future vat-people might give us reason to doubt.

Yitzhak   I don't know. There is still something that's bothering me about this. There being vat-people around during Vatol's lifetime seems to matter. I know Lev thinks it only matters to make the basic problem more salient. But I'm not sure about that.

Lev   If you are Vatol, is the threat of the vat-people that they may attack you? Or infect you with illness? If they are gone there is no more threat?

Yitzhak   Yeah, like "Night of the Living Dead." Here come the vat-people. When you fire, aim for their brains . . . But it seems you're right. It can't matter to my having reason to doubt as Vatol whether I think the vat-people are still around, or whether they came into existence before or after I was born.

Lev   The threat by the vat-people really is . . .

Yitzhak   Yeah, I know, I know. I got it. The threat is I'll have to face the thing that can't possibly be faced. Why don't you drop dead already?

Daniel   Yitzhak! Yitzhak!

Yitzhak   I'm sorry. I apologize, Lev.

Lev   I forgive you, Yitzhak. On the grounds that you are—"*mamish* a crazy man."

Yitzhak   Right.

Daniel   So where are we?

Interlude: memories of Berkeley

Yitzhak   You know, I'm curious about something, Lev. Let me ask you something. What did actually happen in Berkeley? You went home to

France after the spring semester and then you never came back. That was the spring semester we took the peyote. It must have been late in spring. I remember it was a hot sunny day. We were walking up and down Bancroft Way giggling at everything. Then I went off by myself ... That was probably a mistake ... But what happened to you? Was it after that when you went to see the psychiatrist?

Lev   No, no Yitzhak. That was months earlier. Remember it was you who had, *azoi vee mir zugt*, a "bad trip," not I. I did not return to Berkeley. . Enough of sunny California. *Genuck shoyn.* We were very young, Yitzhak.

Yitzhak   "Now as I was young and easy under the apple boughs, about the lilting house and happy as the grass was green, ..., and as I was green and carefree, famous among the barn façades."* Alvin Goldman's version of the poem.[2]—At Berkeley our topic was always epistemology. You and me. Before that, when I was in Brooklyn College, Dean and I, who had philosophized together since we were small children, would talk endlessly about Descartes' skepticism, talked until we "tired the sun with talking, and sent him down the sky."† Then Berkeley. So why didn't you tell me? You said to the psychiatrist that you doubted external reality. Why didn't you say that to me?

Lev   I am sorry, Yitzhak. It was because to your friends you must say only the truth. If it is sayable.

---

* From Dylan Thomas's "Fern Hill" (1946) (with the word "façade" added).
† From the poem "Heraclitus," written by Callimachus around 260 BC, mourning the death of his friend Heraclitus (not the more famous earlier Heraclitus); translation in Corey (1905).

Yitzhak If it is sayable! You know, your kids are so normal. How's that possible? When Eva stayed with us last summer she was an absolute delight. And soon medical school! How proud you must be. But she was always great in science, I remember.

Lev Thank you, Yitzhak. I am remembering Eva. She was very small. This was in France. I think she was not yet in school. But somewhere she picked up about atoms. Perhaps her cousins said something. I was *mamash* afraid to tell her. It may not be as it appears. It is mostly empty space. Of course she did not care in the least. The mind goes about its business. A line I think from Edward Albee.

Yitzhak Have you guys noticed that the biggest philosophers in the world don't have children? Go down a list of eminent philosophers and probably half of them have no kids. And many of these philosophers specialize in Ethics! What do you know about what's good and bad in human life if you've never had any children? I think these philosophers should be locked in a room and forced to read Plato.

Daniel I don't think Plato says much of anything about having children.

Yitzhak I meant it as a punishment.

Pryor's epistemic principle

Daniel Ah. . . . Okay. Good. So where do we stand now? The safety condition suggested by Yitz doesn't seem to do anything for us. It seems at this point, therefore, that the n to n-plus-one principle is correct. And this seems certainly to place a great deal of pressure on the view that as things stand there is no reason to doubt. But here is what I propose, *kinder*. There is a vast literature responding to skepticism about external reality. We should look at some of the main epistemic principles formulated in that literature. We continue to assume that Vatol has reason to doubt. We will be looking to see if there is some plausible epistemic principle that distinguishes us from Vatol, that implies that we have no reason to doubt though he does.

Lev   An excellent plan, Daniel. Let us put that vast literature to good use. But if I may say my feelings on this. Like other professional philosophers I have been taught many arguments and counterarguments on the Cartesian reflection, as if many steps— yes?—as if choreographed steps to dance towards or away from the impact of the reflection. But I believe that none of these arguments will seem as compelling, *Ich mein*, as *honest* as the initial, raw impact of the reflection itself. But let us dance, Daniel. By all means.

Daniel   Good. Good. Okay. We're interested in epistemic *perceptual* principles, that is, principles that tell us, roughly speaking, under what conditions we have reason to trust that our perceptual experience is veridical. Here again there are a plethora of hard issues that I think we should try to skirt, at least for the time being. One question is how perceptual experience relates to belief. Another question is how to draw the line between perception and inference. Let's for now just say that experience "represents" the external world as being a certain way, or that experience "seems to say" that the world is a certain way. I think that's good enough to get this started. And let's say that to "trust" an experience as being veridical is to believe that the world is in fact as the experience represents it as being, that the world is as the experience seems to say it is.

When we talk about a "perceptual principle" we mean a principle that is not merely a corollary of general principles of deductive or inductive reasoning. The perceptual principles establish a *special* presumption in favor of the veridicality of perceptual experience, a presumption that is not merely a corollary of inductive generalizations or reasoning to the best explanation. We are, I take it, in agreement with those many philosophers who have said that reasoning inductively from premises describing subjective experience may perhaps render certain propositions about external reality somewhat probable, but cannot be the basis for knowledge or belief in our sense of outright belief.

Lev   Just as Descartes said in the early Meditations.

Daniel   Yes, perhaps so. But an immediate problem with appealing to perceptual principles is that it seems that Vatol too could appeal to such principles. This doesn't seem to give us the difference we're seeking between us and Vatol.

Yitzhak   I think this depends on how the principles are spelled out.

Daniel   Well, let's start out by considering some standard formulations. I like the formulation in Jim Pryor.[3] Pryor holds that perceptual experience can't be characterized except in terms of its propositional content, and this content is about external reality. So it's not like for the sense-data philosophers, where experience divides up into two components, sense-data that have no propositional content and then a belief that has propositional content about external reality. For Pryor the experience as a whole has propositional content and isn't made up of two separable components, one that has and one that lacks propositional content.

Yitzhak   Of course, a lot of people have been saying that. For example, Searle; and Siegel.[4] That's often the basic idea of an "intentionalist" analysis of perception.

Daniel   Yes, of course. But there are two other points in Pryor, and I think that especially the second is presented by him with exceptional clarity. The first point is that the perceptual principle must not be understood as providing a presumption in favor of the *general* reliability of one's experience, from which one could then make an inference about the veridicality of a specific experience.

Yitzhak   Roger White seems to suggest something like that.[5]

Daniel   Yes. But on Pryor's view it is each experience itself that gives one reason to have a belief in what that experience seems to say. The reason for the belief does not derive from an inference that you make or could make. The epistemic principle says that if you have an experience that represents there being an external object with a certain property, then you thereby have prima-facie reason to believe that there is an external object with that property. The properties that figure in the epistemic principle presumably have to be limited in certain ways, but let's not worry about that for now. The second point is that the reason-conferring role of the experience is to be understood as deriving from a certain phenomenological feature of the experience that Pryor calls its *phenomenal force*.[6]

I understand this to mean that it is in the essential nature of the experience that it in some sense purports to be revelatory of the external facts. Without this it wouldn't be perceptual experience.

Yitzhak   I suppose that another kind of perceptual principle comes out of the "disjunctivism" defended in different forms by people like Martin and McDowell.[7] But I don't really see how that could change anything related to skepticism. It certainly doesn't seem that Vatol's epistemic plight will be ameliorated by disjunctivism. These philosophers apparently think that the disjunctivist formulation makes it easier to accept the kind of perceptual principle given by Pryor. I don't see why that's so.

Lev   That disjunctivism is a part of the mechanism that moves without anything moving with it. Yet Professor McDowell has said that we are "lost" without it. He is half right.

Daniel   You mean we are lost either way . . .

Lev   These philosophers who avow disjunctivism are fanatics of logical form.

Daniel   Why "fanatics," Lev? They are disagreeing with people like Siegel and Pryor about the logical form of veridical experience as compared to the logical form of hallucinatory experiences. They claim that in the veridical case there is an irreducible relation between the perceiver and the object perceived. It may perhaps follow that they do not go along with Wittgenstein's apparent wholesale rejection of the notion of logical form. But many philosophers continue to appeal to something like the "logical form of the facts," at least in some instances.

Lev   I am of the opinion that only a fanatic of logical form could be holding that there is an intelligible difference between "directly confronting the object" in an "irreducible relation" and having an experience that veridically represents an object. This supposed difference gives no difference to the fallibility of perceptual judgments, and gives no difference to the causes required for a veridical experience. But perhaps this is not the occasion to talk more on this.

Daniel   I agree.

Yitzhak   But just to be sure we're carrying on a conversation that disjunctivists could join let's stipulate that by "experience" or "sense experience" we mean whatever can't be introspectively distinguished from veridical perception. Disjunctivists will agree, I think, that in this sense there are sense-experiences in both veridical and non-veridical perception.

Lev   If I may interject a connection between what we have been discussing in Jim Pryor and something said by William James. In the early part of *The Varieties of Religious Experience* William James states that a normal component of perceptual experience is a "sense of presence" or a "sense of reality." And James implies, if I do not make a mistake, that it is possible to have a kind of experience which is like the normal perceptual experience except that this sense of reality is lacking, in other words, a kind of experience which is the normal perceptual experience minus the sense of reality.[8] I am wondering if James's sense of reality is close to Pryor's phenomenal force. Could there be a subtraction of the phenomenal force and leave us still with an experience? Then the perceptual principle of Pryor which we have been discussing would not apply to such an experience.

Daniel Ah, interesting. But I'm not sure that I really understand this. I'm not sure that I can imagine the sort of experience James is describing. It's like seeing a table but minus the sense of the presence of a table? What could that be like?

Lev Yitzhak, I believe you know something about this from what you once described to me about your peyote experience.

Yitzhak I can't go into that. I don't remember that crazy experience.

Daniel Okay, all of this is interesting but I don't think we need to pursue it right now. Perhaps we can agree to adopt in what follows the sort of analysis found in Pryor. The main problem that I think we need to address is that the perceptual principle seems to apply to Vatol. The principle allows him to trust his experience and to believe that he lives in a world in which there are many vat-people. But there may be something odd about that.

Distinction between one-level and two-level cases

Yitzhak I think there *is* something odd about it. Let me try to give an account of a perceptual principle that implies that, whereas we have reason to trust our experience, Vatol doesn't. But I'm afraid that this will be a bit of a story.

Lev I love very much to hear your whole story, Yitzhak, but if I may interject just to keep our bearings, *azoy vee mir zugt* [as one says]. I do not mean to turn the blade inside you, but I think you have already conceded that we ourselves might be in no better philosophical situation than Vatol if we believe that vat-people existed a trillion years ago or even if we consider it likely that there will be vat-people a trillion years in the future. And I am understanding that you are not now attempting to ameliorate those problems for your view.

Yitzhak That's quite right. I don't know at present what to say about those questions. My task at present is to explain what would be the relevant epistemic difference between Vatol and us, where Vatol believes that there are many contemporaneous vat-people and we, I'm now supposing, do not take seriously the prospect that vat-people have ever existed or ever will exist.

Lev Then go forward, my son. *Luz herrin!*

Yitzhak The perceptual principle creates a defeasible presumption in favor of your trusting each of your experiences. It seems that there are two very different ways in which the presumption can be defeated. We can, I think, distinguish between *one-level* and *two-level* examples.[9] In a one-level example you have a set of experiences that, if taken to be veridical, provide evidence in favor of the truth of some proposition *p,* and you have another set of experiences that, if taken to be veridical, provide evidence against *p.* In some one-level cases there will be no resolution as to whether *p* is true; in other cases one set of experiences, because of its greater extensiveness or coherence, will trump the other set. In a two-level example, although you may have no experiences that provide evidence for or against p, you have experiences that, if taken to be veridical, provide evidence that your sensory faculties cannot be trusted with respect to p.

Suppose that one morning you walk out of your house and you seem to see that your lawn is red and the passing fire engine is green. You have had in the past a far more extensive set of experiences that, if taken to be veridical, provide overwhelming evidence that the lawn is really green and the fire engine red. This is a one-level example in which the presumption in favor of your current experience may be defeated; that is, you may have reason not to trust your current experience.

Here is a two-level example. Suppose your eye-doctor tells you that the drops he put in your eyes will have the effect for several hours of making you see red objects as green and green objects as red. When you leave his office a car passes that appears to be red. Although you had no prior evidence that the car is not really red, you will reasonably doubt that your current experience of its being red is veridical.

There is a striking difference between how the defeasibility concept operates in one-level and two-level examples. In one-level examples the presumptive veridicality of the defeated experience retains the power to undermine at least to some small extent the presumptive veridicality of the defeater experience or the credibility of the beliefs coming out of that experience; that is not the case in two-level examples. In the one-level example just mentioned the presumption of veridicality of your experience of the grass as red may be defeated by the general beliefs that came out of your earlier experience—I mean the general belief that grass is never red—but the presumptive veridicality of the later experience does to some extent undermine those beliefs. If prior to experiencing the grass as red the probability was P that grass is never red, it's clear that after you experience the grass as red this probability is P minus epsilon, for some epsilon however small. In the two-level example about the eye-drops it doesn't work that way at all. The presumptive veridicality of your experience of the car as red is defeated by the beliefs that came out of your earlier experience of getting the drops and hearing what the doctor said about the drops, and the presumptive veridicality of the later experience does not undermine those beliefs one iota: the probability of the truth of those beliefs remains exactly the same after you experience the car as red. You don't reason, "Since there is the presumption that this experience I'm now having is veridical, that's evidence that I never took the eye drops."

It's not obvious why in two-level examples the defeated experience seems to completely lose its presumption of veridicality; it's as if the presumption in favor of the defeated experience is not just trumped but completely obliterated by the power of the defeater experience. We can bring this out more vividly by considering a case in which the doctor tells you that the drops reverse red-green perception only half the time. Suppose you believe this. Then when you experience the car as red you will assign a probability of .5 that it is red and .5 that it is green. Why? Why not trust your experience and say that this is one of the cases in which the drops had no effect? Contrast this with a one-level case in which a doctor tells you that there is a .5 probability that a certain medicine you're taking will have the effect of turning your urine red and a .5 probability of turning it green. If you experience it as red you simply trust your experience—very different from the two-level case.

There is a related point. In a one-level case lottery-style probabilities don't seem in general to defeat the presumption of veridicality. Suppose you're in a lottery with a one in a hundred chance of winning. If you win, you're supposed to get a red envelope in the mail. When an envelope comes and you experience it as red—I mean in good lighting, with time to carefully look at it, and so on—then you simply trust your experience: you won the lottery. The fact that there was a 99 percent lottery-style probability that you wouldn't win does not defeat the presumption that your experience of winning is veridical. Only non-lottery-style probabilities can undermine the presumption in one-level cases—for example, the high probability that green things do not suddenly turn red. Not so in two-level cases. Suppose that the drops given to you are randomly chosen from a hundred specimens, ninety-nine of which produce color distortions. The lottery-style probability of your getting the distorting drops is enough for you to distrust your experience almost completely.

Daniel   Of course the distinction between lottery-style improbabilities and—what should we call it?—weird events? unnatural events?—is hard to clarify. But it does seem to figure in much of our reasoning. Hawthorne's book really brings this home.[10]

Yitzhak   So our first task is to say something about what perceptual principles are at work in this distinction between one-level and two-level cases. It's the two-level cases that are harder to understand, and these are the cases that are most relevant to the skeptical issues we're talking about. I'm going to try to formulate a principle that applies to such cases.

Interlude: Talmudic connections

Lev   Please. If I may first offer a comment about the distinction you were just mentioning between lottery-style and other improbabilities. That distinction is, I believe, the underlying *sevara* of the distinction, the *chiluk* in the Gemara between *ruba d' eesa kaman* and *ruba d'lessa kaman*.* If there is found a piece of meat that might have come out of one of ten butchers, nine of whom are kosher, this is only a *ruba d' eesa kaman* in favor of its being kosher, merely a lottery-style probability. Yes? But if a women comes into town with a newborn baby on her arms, this is a *ruba d'lessa kaman* in favor of her being the mother, for it would be unnatural if she is not the mother.

Yitzhak   I think that may be a pretty good model for the Gemara's distinction, Lev.

Lev   The distinction, if I may add, seems to show itself in the Gemara even where *rov* is not being in the spotlight. We see this, I am thinking, in the Mishnah in *Bava* Kama 21b which maintains that if a dog jumps off the roof and damages a utensil the dog's owner is liable. The Mishnah did not specify any conditions on how

---

* A "chiluk" in the Talmud is a distinction relevant to the law; a "sevara" for the *chiluk* is its rationale. The distinction between *ruba d' eesa kaman* and *ruba d'lessa kaman* is explained in the text that follows. These are two variants of a Talmudic principle of evidence called "rov," which means "majority (of cases)" (see, e.g., *Hullin* 11a).

large an area there is for the dog to jump onto. Conceive of a long, long roof abutting a very long yard, and there is on the yard a single small utensil. It must be manifest that we are not talking about a bad dog that is aiming to land on the utensil, but a dog that jumps and lands randomly on the utensil. The Mishnah implies that there is liability in this case. Why is this so when it is as all can see unlikely that the dog would land on the utensil? This question perplexes more when we keep in our minds that the Gemara following the Mishnah explains that if the dog does not jump away from the wall but rather falls on a utensil close to the wall, then there is no liability, because dogs do not normally fall. If the improbability of the dog's falling is the basis for exemption from liability, why not the same be said for the improbability of the jumping dog's randomly striking the isolated utensil? We are given no reason to think that the measure of the first improbability is greater than the second. The explanation, I am promoting this, is that the first improbability is merely a lottery-style improbability, and the Gemara is informing us that the owner is not permitted to rely on that kind of improbability.[11]

Daniel   That's interesting, Lev.

Lev   Yitzhak, did you say before that I gave a "model"? That would gratify me. For I have been told that at MIT if graduate students present an argument without an accompanying logical model they are immediately removed from the program.

Daniel   Yes, they are kicked out, together with all their friends and relatives.

Lev   Yet there remain some philosophers, such as Saul Kripke, who because of their ignorance of logic persist in presenting philosophical arguments without the help of models.

Daniel   That's true. I think that out of compassion for philosophers like Kripke we should try to get by without models when we do normal philosophy.

Yitzhak   I don't think either of you understand what modeling something in philosophy is supposed to accomplish.

Lev   Yitzhak, perhaps you can instruct us on this by modeling modeling for us.

Yitzhak   Modeling modeling. That reminds me of something I was thinking about a few minutes ago. You know, Jim Pryor's work may have a bearing on the issue of priors in Bayesian theory. How will this sound? "Prior to Pryor priors were prioritized differently." I think there is no possible world in which a language like English is spoken. The existence of English is a counterexample to the modal principle that whatever is actual is possible. That and child rearing.

Lev   I will ask you two erudite scholars a challenge. Which philosopher criticized another philosopher by saying that he was arguing like a "mere mathematician"?

Daniel   Is that from Kripke's "Substitutional Quantification"?

Lev   Leibniz! Leibniz said it.

Yitzhak   No kidding. Who did he say it to?

Lev   To Williamson.

Yitzhak Come on.

Lev To Clarke. In the Leibniz–Clarke debate.

Yitzhak Really? That's interesting . . . Okay, let me get back to the point I was making about the difference between one-level and two-level cases.

Daniel Yitz, I have an idea about that difference. It seems to me analogous to the *chiluk* in the Gemara between *hakchashah* and *hazamah*.[12] In the case of *hakchashah* one set of witnesses testify to the truth of the proposition *p*, and then another set of witnesses testifies that not-*p*. In this case the contradictory testimonies nullify each other. In the case of *hazamah* one set of witnesses testifies that *p*, and then another set of witnesses testifies that the first witnesses were not in the position to testify about *p*. For example, the first witnesses say that Reuven committed a theft at a certain place and time, and the second witnesses say that the first witnesses were at a different place at that time and therefore they could not have seen whether Reuven did the theft. In the case of *hazamah* the *halachah* is that we believe the second witnesses. Why is this? I think that the *mefarshim* [commentators] explain it along the following lines. If witnesses testify that *p*, this creates a defeasible presumption that *p*. But witnesses cannot be credited as testifying to the reliability of their own testimony or to the fulfillment of conditions needed for the reliability of their testimony. Therefore, when the second witnesses impugn the reliability of the first witnesses' testimony, there is no testimony to contradict them. So the testimony of the second witnesses stands, and the testimony of the first witnesses is thrown out. That's analogous to the two-level cases. An experience cannot testify to its own reliability. So when, in the two-level case, one set of experiences impugns the reliability of another set, the former experiences are believed and the latter are thrown out.

Yitzhak   That's really a nice try, Danny. Of course once you start bringing in *halachic* details, which aren't always intuitive, there are obvious problems. For example, the *halachah* is that two witnesses have as much credibility as a hundred.[13] So in the case of *hakchashah* if two witnesses say that *p* and a hundred say that not-*p*, they are all equally nullified. That doesn't fit what we wanted to say in the one-level case where the numerous experiences of green grass may overwhelm a single experience as if of red grass.

Daniel   Of course you're right that once we bring in *halachic* details that don't seem intuitive the analogy won't be helpful. But is there an example in which we intuitively want to say something about a case of *hakchashah* that doesn't match our intuitions about one-level cases, or an example in which we intuitively want to say something about a case of *hazamah* that doesn't match our intuitions about two-level cases?

Yitzhak   I'm not sure. First of all, despite your explanation I'm not at all sure that the intuitive thing to say in the case of *hazamah* is that we believe the second witnesses more than the first. But, also, consider the following example. You are an eye-doctor administering the drops to yourself. It happens that the drops that affect color vision are red, and there are some other green drops that have no effect on color vision. You choose the drops that appear red, administer them, and then they appear green. In this example what the second experience says, namely, that the drops are green, *is* evidence against what the first experience says. Nevertheless, it seems clear that we will trust the first experience, not the second. So this is an example analogous to a case of *hakchashah* combined with *hazamah*. What is the *halachah* in that kind of case? Lev! What's the answer? *Nu!* What's the answer?

Lev   I believe that the *mefarshim* have disputed over it.

Yitzhak   I think you're right.[14] An example would be where the first set of witnesses testifies that Reuven committed a theft in the Bronx on Tuesday and the second set testifies that all day Tuesday they were together in Brooklyn both with the first witnesses, who therefore couldn't have seen any theft in the Bronx, and also with Reuven, who they say didn't commit any theft. If the analogy to two-level cases works intuitively, then we ought to say that in this kind of example the intuition is that we believe the second witnesses and throw out the first witnesses. Is that really the intuition? I doubt it. So it may not be that easy to draw a good comparison between the testimony of witnesses and the so-called testimony of the senses.

Lev   Very good. I think you are right. We would have to delve into this further. But perhaps you should now get back to formulating the principle that you said would distinguish us from Vatol.

The "non-circularity" condition

Yitzhak   So let me get back to two-level cases and the special way in which the presumption of perceptual veridicality seems to get defeated in such cases. I think we need to say that there are irreducible principles of defeasibility at work here. We agreed—as I think most philosophers would—that the a priori presumption of veridicality is an irreducible principle not derivable from general principles of inductive reasoning. I think we have to say the same for the principles that define in what cases the presumption is defeated. We can't expect to derive those principles from something else.

Daniel   I think there is a thought similar to that in Alston, something to the effect that our doxastic practices include both principles for acquiring beliefs and principles for correcting those beliefs.[15]

Yitzhak   Yeah. Okay. So let me try to sketch what the relevant defeasibility principles are. I think the most basic idea is this: *If one has evidence that there is a certain kind of perceptual defect that some people suffer from, then the presumption that a given experience is veridical can play no role in defending the veridicality of that experience against the possibility that the experience is caused by that perceptual defect.* Let's call that "the non-circularity" principle. Suppose that in the example where the drops have a 50-50 chance of causing red-green reversal, you reason as follows: "Here is a red car (as I can plainly see), and it appears red to me, so I can conclude that the drops have not adversely affected my vision." That would violate the non-circularity principle.

In applying the non-circularity principle there is a subtlety that has to be noted. The principle says that, if there is prior evidence of a perceptual defect that might be affecting an experience, then the experience's presumptive veridicality can play no role in defending its veridicality against that possible defect. But in some examples the mere fact that the experience *occurs* can play that role. Consider

again the initial eye-drops example, where the drops were supposed
to work all the time. Suppose that your friend is with you at the
doctor's office. Before you get the drops you seem to perceive that his
tie is red, and now that the drops have been administered you still
seem to see that his tie is red. The occurrence of the later experience
is evidence of its veridicality and evidence that you misheard your
doctor (or that his declaration was false), since, if the drops worked,
it's extremely unlikely that you would experience the tie as red
(it's extremely unlikely that its color changed from red to green).
But there is no appeal here to the presumptive veridicality of the
experience. The appeal is rather to the fact that you are having a
certain experience as if of a red tie in conjunction with various
accepted facts about your friend's tie. You are, in other words, not
appealing to the presumptive veridicality of the experience, but
rather you're reasoning to the simplest or best explanation of why
such an experience would occur. We agreed earlier that, if you start
out with just the totality of your subjective experience, reasoning to
the best explanation can't provide you with reason to believe in an
external reality, that is, to believe outright or to claim knowledge. But
in the present example you already have all kinds of background
beliefs about external reality, including beliefs about the color of
your friend's tie, the unlikelihood of the color changing, and so on.
Given that background it may well be that reasoning to the best
explanation generates a reason to believe that the tie is red. But the
crucial point is that the non-circularity principle prevents you from
appealing to the presumptive veridicality of the experience of red.

Let me try to put all of this in more general terms. Let's say that
a "delusional circumstance" is a kind of circumstance such that

people who are in it suffer a substantial likelihood of having non-veridical experiences with respect to certain propositions. Let's call those experiences "vulnerable" relative to that kind of circumstance. In the eye-drops example the delusional circumstance is getting the drops, and the experiences that are vulnerable relative to this circumstance are experiences that something is red or that something is green.

Now the general formulation of the non-circularity principle is very roughly this: *If you have experiences which, if taken as veridical, provide you with evidence that there is a certain kind of delusional circumstance, then you cannot trust experiences that are vulnerable relative to that circumstance until you provide non-circular evidence that you are not in that circumstance, that is, evidence that does not derive from vulnerable experiences.*

This is obviously very rough. First of all, it needs eventually to be clarified what exactly is meant by "veridical," and how to draw a distinction between hallucinations, illusions, and various other kinds of perceptual errors. But I think that for our immediate purposes the idea of a "delusional circumstance" is probably clear enough. For example, it's understood, I think, that marriage doesn't qualify as a delusional circumstance in the relevant sense.

Daniel   Which of your ex-wives will agree with that, Yitz?

Yitzhak   Yeah. Right. More important—and this is in fact *extremely* important—is the point that a number of things have to be filled in about strengths of evidence, and about how substantial the likelihood is of having a non-veridical experience in the delusional circumstance. But I think we have enough to make the main point I'm driving at, which is what the relevant epistemic difference is between Vatol and us. The difference is that Vatol has evidence that there is actually a delusional circumstance that people suffer from and that he could possibly be suffering from, and we have no such evidence. The delusional circumstance is of course being a vat-person. And the experiences that are vulnerable relative to that circumstance are *all* perceptual experiences. This is why Vatol has no hope of extricating himself from his reasons to doubt external reality. But none of that applies to our situation.

Daniel's challenges to Yitzhak's view

Daniel I'm confused about this, Yitz. I think, in fact, that I have four distinct questions about your position.

Yitzhak Four questions? That's reminding me of a *Seder* and making me hungry. *Matzah! Matzah!*

Daniel Here is my first question. I have often had the experience of seeming to read reports of the following sort: "Many millions of people were hallucinating their entire lives because they were attached to this master computer called the Matrix; only a few heroic people were outside the Matrix trying to free the others from their hallucinations." Now if that were the *only* relevant experience given to me, that would be evidence that I live in a world together with numerous life-long hallucinators. So how am I different from Vatol? Of course that is *not* the only relevant experience I have. I also have the experience of seeming to read that these are merely reports about what is taking place in a fictional movie. But the same holds for Vatol. He has other relevant experiences too, for example, the experience of seeming to walk down the street, which, if believed, proves he is not a vat-person. Perhaps my question can be made more forceful by considering an example in which, after reading the report about the Matrix, and not suspecting that it is merely fiction, I come to believe that there is actually the delusive circumstance of being in the Matrix. Shouldn't the non-circularity principle then forbid me from trusting my subsequent experience of seeming to read that the Matrix is merely fiction, since this experience is vulnerable relative to the circumstance of being in the Matrix?

Yitzhak   That's very good, Danny. I've never thought of that kind of example. But I think something I want to say later might answer it, so let's hear your next question, and we'll come back to this one.

Lev   If I may please interject a comment about the Matrix, though not directly relevant. The people in the Matrix, unlike the vat-people, are able to communicate with each other. They are deluded only about physical states, not about each other's minds. This is no great tragedy. Only communication with other persons is deeply important. This is why Berkeley's denial of matter is merely silly, not horrific. Horrific is Hilary Putnam's suggestion that, even if I am a brain-in-a-vat, I do not have mistaken beliefs about the existence of thoughts and feelings in other persons.

Daniel   Don't you think that Wittgenstein might have said something like that?

Lev What are you saying, Daniel? What are you saying? How could Wittgenstein hold such a thing?

Daniel Okay, okay, let's definitely not get sidetracked into Wittgenstein exegesis ...

Yitzhak Here's Wittgenstein on behaviorism: "My position has often been confused with behaviorism. I hope my present remarks will not be misinterpreted. *There is nothing but behavior.*"

Lev That is nonsense, Yitzhak! Have you not read Kripke?

Yitzhak In fact, I never understood a word of Wittgenstein until I read Kripke. Now I do understand a word.

Daniel Okay, okay, please, let's not go down that road. So now, here is my second question, Yitzhak. In the case of the eye-drops I have one set of experiences that, if believed, provide evidence of the delusional circumstance. And I have another set of experiences that are vulnerable relative to that delusional circumstance. I must therefore not trust the latter experiences. In Vatol's case, however, the very experiences that, if believed, provide evidence of the delusional circumstance also provide evidence that Vatol is not a vat-person. He has the experience, for example, of seeming to read a report about vat-people in a newspaper. If that experience is believed, he is assured he is not a vat-person, since vat-people cannot really read reports in newspapers. So how can this experience be evidence that he may be a vat-person?

Yitzhak I think the answer is that you have to divide up the content of the experience.

Lev   *Palginan dibura.**

Yitzhak   Yeah, it is a little like *palginan dibura*. We can extract
two different propositions from the total propositional content of
Vatol's experience of seeming to read the report. One proposition is
that there is a report about the existence of vat-people; the other
proposition is that Vatol read a report. The first proposition prohibits
him from appealing to the second proposition because that would
violate the non-circularity principle.

Daniel   Okay. I'm not really sure that I understand why it should
work that way. But I think that my third question may get to the heart
of the matter. In the eye-drops example the experience that provided
evidence of the delusional circumstance was not itself vulnerable to
that circumstance. In Vatol's case, however, his experience of reading
the report is itself vulnerable to the delusional circumstance
of being a vat-person. Why, then, should he believe that he has
really read any such report? And, if he does not believe that he
has read such a report, why should he believe that there are any
vat-people?

Lev   *ha-peh she-asar/ha-peh she-hitir.†*

---

* Literally: "We divide words." As an illustration, suppose that Jones testifies in court, "Smith
committed adultery with my wife." Assuming that a person cannot incriminate his wife, the
testimony as a whole cannot be accepted by the court. The Talmudic principle of *palginan
dibura* would allow the court to accept the part of the testimony that says that Smith
committed adultery, leaving out the part that says it was with Jones's wife. See, e.g., *Sanhedrin*
9b–10a; *Yevomot* 25a.

† Literally: "The mouth that prohibits is the mouth that permits." As an illustration, according
to Talmudic law someone who borrows money is normally not believed to have paid it back
unless he has evidence in the form of a document or witnesses. But suppose the claimant has
no evidence that a loan was made. If the defendant admits that he took the loan but claims
to have paid it back, that claim is believed: if he is believed about the loan (*hapeh she-assar*),
he must be believed about the payment (*hapeh she-hitir*). See, e.g., Kesuvos 16a, 18a.

Daniel That's right. It is like *ha-peh she-asar/ha-peh she-hitir*. If his vulnerable experiences of reading a report can be trusted to condemn him to a world in which there is this delusional circumstance, then he should be able to trust those vulnerable experiences to exonerate him from being a subject of such delusions.

Yitzhak I understand the question. And it's obviously a good point. Let me first reiterate something. I regard these defeasibility principles as being irreducible, as being part of a kind of irreducible "logic of perception" that can't be derived from any other principles. I'm trying to elicit what these principles are by looking at examples.

Yitzhak's stringent response to "entering a loop"

Yitzhak (continuing) Now, let's say that someone "enters a loop" if he has a set of experiences that, when taken as veridical, provide evidence that there is a certain delusional circumstance relative to which those very experiences are vulnerable. If I am Vatol, I enter a loop in this sense. I can then go *le-chumra* [stringently] or *le-kula* [leniently].* To go *le-chumra*, I argue as follows: "If I trust my experience, then I believe there are numerous vat-people. That being the case, I cannot trust my experience. So if I start out trusting my experience, I wind up not trusting my experience. So I cannot trust my experience." To go *le-kula* I argue as follows: "If I do not trust my

---

* When the application of a Talmudic law prohibiting some action is questionable, in some cases the question is resolved stringently (*le-chumra*) and the action is prohibited, in some cases leniently (*le-kula)* and the action is permitted.

experience, then I have no reason to believe that there are vat-people. That being the case, I can trust my experience. So if I start out not trusting my experience, I wind up trusting my experience. So I can trust my experience." Now it's true that my earlier formulation of the non-circularity principle does not immediately tell us what to say about the situation of entering a loop. We have agreed, however, that Vatol has reason to doubt. We see, therefore, that when Vatol enters the loop he must go *le-chumra*. Vatol must doubt all of his perceptual experiences while at the same time doubting that there are vat-people.

Let me give another kind of example of entering a loop. This is an embellishment of an example I once heard from Adam Leite. I'm camping in the Catskills for several days, completely isolated from other people and from the news. I come to a trail in the forest. I once saw scrawled on a sign on a trail in the Catskills, "No way round, or under, or through."—Actually, I wrote it.—Anyway, in this story I'm telling you, I get on this trail, and it leads me to the small Chasidic town of Ployderville. Entering the town I find utter mayhem. Cars are crashed against buildings with their occupants unconscious. All over people are lying unconscious in streets, in stores, in houses. Two yarmulkes uprooted from fallen Jews are carried momentarily in the wind like headless blackbirds. Many unfortunate women are sprawled immodestly on the ground with their bare wrists exposed. Or even their bare elbows.

Lev   *Chas ve-shalom!*

Yitzhak   Right. There are a number of different newspapers in the gutter, including of course the Jewish Daily Forward. I pick it up and

it says it was dropped from a helicopter because the authorities
haven't determined yet how to deal with the Ployderville situation.
The report in the newspaper says that there is a completely new form
of neural virus in Ployderville that invariably and immediately
afflicts anyone who enters the center of the town, where I'm in fact
standing reading the newspaper. The speculation is that the virus is
caused by fumes coming from sewage containing detritus that is
completely free of essential non-glatt-kosher ingredients. Anyone
who contracts the virus collapses to the ground and suffers a
prolonged sequence of completely lucid hallucinatory experiences
that cohere with his real past life. While this is going on the victim
carries on audible conversations with his hallucinated companions.
Victims often have the hallucination of reading and hearing
complicated reports of various physical and mental aberrations.
The psychological mechanisms that determine the details of the
hallucinations are similar to that of dreams, coming from the
victim's unconscious, but in this case there are completely lucid and
coherent hallucinations. Since a number of radios are on in town
discussing the Ployderville disaster, and since the hallucinations
are controlled by unconscious processes, and the victims, many of
whom occasionally open their eyes, are somewhat receptive to their
environment on an unconscious level, the victims' hallucinations
will sometimes incorporate fairly accurate facts about there being a
scourge of hallucinations in Ployderville. That's the report I read in
the newspaper.

After reading this I quickly make my way out of town and
back into the forest. Or do I? Am I really lying on the ground in
Ployderville hallucinating? Here we have an example of my having

entered a loop. If I trust my experiences of how people are behaving in Ployderville, and trust my experience of reading what appears to be an authoritative report in the newspaper about the virus, then I have evidence that there is this delusional circumstance caused by the virus. But these experiences are themselves vulnerable to that delusional circumstance. It seems to me that in this situation I cannot trust any of my experiences, including the experiences that are evidence of a delusional circumstance. I must suspend my belief about whether I have really left Ployderville or am lying there hallucinating, while at the same time suspending my belief about whether there is any delusion-making virus in Ployderville.

I need to emphasize that I'm not getting into probability issues. There is a nice paper by Egan and Elga about an example of entering a memory loop in which one is trying to decide whether to trust one's memory of having been told by one's physician that one's memory cannot be trusted.[16] Egan and Elga attempt a Bayesian analysis to arrive at a probability that one is correctly remembering what the doctor said. Now I think it doubtful that in the example of Ployderville, and even more clearly in the example of Vatol, there are any sensible prior probabilities with which to attempt a Bayesian calculation. I am, in any case, not concerned at present with probabilities. Our question is whether Vatol has reason to believe (to believe outright, to claim to know) the sorts of propositions about his physical environment that we ordinarily believe. My assumption is that he has such a reason only if his experiences are presumptively veridical. And I'm claiming that entering the loop defeats that presumption, so he has no reason to believe those propositions. He has reason to doubt, but we, who do not enter a loop, do not have reason to doubt.

Yitzhak's Austinian answer to the problem of dreams

Daniel   But Yitz, this leads immediately to my fourth and most obvious question. You compared the hallucinations in Ploydervillle to dreams. Well, we dream. So why have we not entered a loop?

Yitzhak   That is indeed the obvious question. I'll try to answer it in a minute. But I'm interested, what did you think the answer was to the problem of dreaming? That's of course a perennial problem that arises without any thoughts about Vatol or Ployderville. It's in fact somewhat controversial whether dreams do consist of delusive perceptual experiences, but I'm inclined to go along with you in addressing the dreaming problem in its traditional form.[17] We'll assume that dreams count as a delusive circumstance. So apart from worries about what my view implies, what did you think the answer was to the problem?

Daniel   I thought Moore suggested an answer.

Yitzhak   Really? Moore's view, as explained by Pryor, seems to be that you can establish that you are not dreaming by appealing to such facts as that you are now walking down the street (in conjunction with the fact that dreamers do not walk down streets).[18] This view seems to absurdly deny the non-circularity principle: since a person can dream that he is walking down the street, your experience as if of walking down the street is evidently vulnerable to the delusional circumstance of dreaming. So it seems absurd to appeal to that experience to show that you're not dreaming. Appealing to the fact that you are walking down the street to show that you are not dreaming seems like appealing, after you took the drops, to the fact that the drops are really green (as they now appear) to show that you didn't take red drops. In neither case does it seem that you can reasonably appeal to experiences that are vulnerable with respect to a certain delusional circumstance to show that you are not in that circumstance.

Let me be clear that I am always assuming a distinction between cases in which there is, and cases in which there isn't, empirical evidence of a relevant delusional circumstance. In the latter cases, I am quite happy with Pryor's position. If we ignore the delusional circumstance of dreams, my experience that seems to say I'm standing here gives me reason to believe I'm standing here, and the fact that I'm standing here while experiencing myself standing here, gives me reason to believe that my experience is veridical. This is in contrast to the suggestion in White that we start in the other direction: I have some kind of a priori basis for the general belief that my experiences are veridical, and I can then infer from my current experience that I'm now standing here. Now I'm not really sure that I see any big-deal difference between Pryor's direction of argument and White's, but Pryor's sounds a bit better to my ears. So I have no problem with the kind of argument he wants to give about cases in which we are not addressing empirical evidence of our being in a delusional circumstance.

But the problem is that he seems to want to apply the argument to show we are not dreaming. Since there is empirical evidence that people dream maybe about 25 percent of the time, this is surely empirical evidence of a relevant delusional circumstance. And to suggest, as Pryor seems to be doing, that I can show I'm not dreaming by appealing to the fact that I'm now standing here seems an absurd violation of the non-circularity constraint.

Daniel I agree that Pryor's interpretation of Moore, if we got it right, seems to present an unattractive view. But I had thought Moore meant something else. I never quite formulated it in these terms, but I thought that Moore was in effect saying that when you enter a loop you go *le-kula*. The position might be put like this: My only reason for believing that people (including me) dream while they sleep depends on my trusting my perceptual experiences of physical facts about myself and other people. For example, I perceive that I lie down in bed at night and close my eyes, and then I find myself in that bed in the morning while remembering intervening experiences that represent events that could not have occurred in that bed. And I perceive other people sleeping, and also perceive their reports of their dreams while they were asleep. Apart from those experiences I would not even have evidence that there is such a thing as going to sleep, let alone that there is some general distinction between waking experience and dream experience. It makes no sense therefore for me to appeal to those experiences as evidence against the veridicality of those very experiences. Those experiences—the experiences that teach me that people dream while they sleep—must be exempt from any doubt arising from the fact that people dream while they sleep. But there is nothing special about those experiences: they are simply experiences of the external world. So all such experiences must be exempt from any doubt arising from the fact that people dream while they sleep. The presumptive veridicality of my current experience of walking down the street is not at all undermined by the fact that people dream while they sleep.

So it does seem, now that you've introduced these terms, that the answer to the dreaming problem must be that when we enter a loop we go *le-kula*. If I doubt my perceptual experience in general, then I have no reason to believe that there is any such delusional circumstance as dreaming, in which case I have no reason to doubt my perceptual experience in general. So if I doubt it, I have no reason to doubt it. So I have no reason to doubt it. But if you're right that we go *le-chumra* when we enter a loop, this answer to the dreaming problem is not available to us.

Yitzhak   Given our assumption that Vatol has reason to doubt, it seems to follow that we do go *le-chumra*. But the question now is why the delusional circumstance of dreaming doesn't put us in essentially the same situation as Vatol. Why haven't we entered a loop? I'll try to answer this.

I'm drawing here from some work by Adam Leite on a view presented in J. L. Austin's lectures.[19] Austin's view, as explained by Leite, is that I can determine that I am not dreaming by appealing to the fact that my experience is lucid and coherent, in contrast to the experience during dreams that has a dream-like quality. I am assuming that when I dream I have no experience that deludes me about the phenomenological character of my dream experience. My current lucid and coherent experience is therefore not vulnerable to the delusional circumstance of dreaming.

Daniel   I don't understand. I'm willing to waive any problem with the assumption that you cannot be deluded in judging that your current experience is lucid. But what reason . . .

Lev Why are you so quick to waive that problem, Daniel? Do not people in general believe that they are awake when they dream?

Daniel It doesn't follow that when they dream they believe that their experiences are lucid and coherent. Perhaps they do *not* believe that their experiences are *not* lucid and coherent, but that doesn't mean that they mistakenly believe that their experiences *are* lucid and coherent. When I am awake I can consider the question, "Am I now lucid and coherent?" and I'm disposed to answer the question in the affirmative. That may be impossible for dreamers. It may be impossible for them to make a considered and reflective judgment that they are lucid and coherent.

Yitzhak I think that may be right, but we need to clear something up, or at least touch on it. I previously said that a "delusional circumstance" is a kind of circumstance such that people who are in it suffer a substantial likelihood of having non-veridical experiences with respect to certain propositions, and that such experiences are "vulnerable" relative to that kind of circumstance. On that formulation only *experiences* can be vulnerable to a delusional circumstance. Beliefs or judgments can't be vulnerable on this formulation. I'm certainly not trying to give a general account of when one has reason to worry about making mistakes in one's judgments, for example, when one has reason to worry that one is making a mistake because of prejudice. As I've said, I'm suggesting that there are special epistemic principles with regard to perceptual experience, and those are the principles that I've been trying to formulate. So let's suppose that dreamers *do* mistakenly judge that their experiences are lucid and coherent. It's not clear how that would affect my argument unless it's held, as I suppose Locke might, that we have a kind of "inner" experience that says that we are, or aren't, in a lucid state. If that were so, then it could be held that dreamers have delusive inner experiences of being lucid, so that our own experience of being lucid is vulnerable to the delusional circumstance of dreaming. But how plausible is it to suppose that dreamers have delusional inner experiences of their mental states? Even if one makes the notion of "inner experience" somewhat more innocuous by associating it with "acts of introspection," I don't think it's very plausible to suppose that dreamers have delusive acts of introspection. So it seems that even if dreamers do somehow wind up in some sense believing falsely that they are lucid and coherent, that won't make any of our experiences vulnerable, and there seems therefore to be no argument along the lines I've been developing against our believing that we are lucid and coherent, and therefore not dreaming. And it does indeed seem intuitive to me that if our waking beliefs that we are lucid and coherent stem from our introspection, whereas the dreamers' mistaken beliefs that they are lucid and coherent do not stem from introspection, then their mistaken beliefs give us no reason to worry that our beliefs are mistaken.

Daniel   I'm not sure if I follow all of that, but as I started to say, I'm willing to waive any problem with the assumption that you cannot be deluded in judging that your current experience is lucid. I have a more obvious concern: What reason do you have to believe that dream experiences cannot be lucid, that they must be phenomenologically different from waking experience? Of course, there may be scientific evidence that this is so, based in part perhaps on certain neurological findings. But how can you appeal to any such findings? The obvious problem is that you may have merely dreamt that there are such findings. Suppose you remember having lucidly experienced reading a number of authoritative reports about such findings in the library. Putting aside possible doubts about the correctness of your memory of your past experiences, which we have not been considering, the question I'm asking is how you can rule out that you had a lucid dream of reading authoritative reports in the library saying that dreams cannot be lucid. If we're saying, as against Pryor's apparent position, that it is circular to simply appeal to the fact that you experience being in a library, to show that you are not dreaming, how could it be less circular to appeal to your experience of reading reports in the library? If you might be dreaming that you are in a library, you might also be dreaming that you are reading a report in the library. It is therefore circular for you to claim that dreams cannot be lucid on the basis of having read reports to that effect.

Yitzhak   But listen to what I'm saying. There are two distinct epistemic steps here. The first step is to determine what kinds of delusional circumstances are found in the world, that is, what kinds of perceptual delusions people actually suffer from. The second step is to determine with respect to a given experience whether it is vulnerable to some delusional circumstance. At the first step, the delusions-identifying step, one does not concern oneself as yet with issues of circularity. One provisionally takes all of one's experiences as veridical and thereby constructs one's most plausible theory of what delusional circumstances are in the world. At the second step one applies the results of the first step to one's current experience, and one must then respect the non-circularity constraint, which says that an experience that is vulnerable to a certain delusional circumstance cannot be appealed to in showing that one is not in that circumstance. At the first step Vatol identifies the delusional circumstance of being a vat-person; this is a kind of delusion that, at the first step, he takes many people to be suffering from. He therefore cannot appeal at the second step to the fact that, say, he is walking down the street to show that he is not a vat-person, since the experience of walking down the street is vulnerable to the delusions suffered by vat-people. The additional twist in this example is that Vatol entered a loop, in that even the experiences that led in the first step to identifying the vat-delusional-circumstance is vulnerable to that circumstance; hence, Vatol is left without reason to even believe that there are vat-people, and without reason to believe anything else that comes out of his experience. All of those beliefs must be suspended.

Now contrast Vatol's situation with our situation in regard to dreaming. I'm assuming that we have empirical evidence that dreams cannot be lucid and coherent. So that is our conclusion at the first step. The second step is to consider what reason I now have to believe that I'm not in the dream-delusional circumstance. I can do that without violating the non-circularity constraint, insofar as I assume I cannot be deluded about my currently lucid state.

Daniel   So are you saying that at the first step we go *le-kula* and at the second step *le-chumra*?

Yitzhak   Maybe it could be looked at like that, but that makes it sound arbitrary. The point is, how else could it be at the first step? Consider the question quickly dismissed by Descartes in the first *Meditation*. People are perceptually deluded in certain ways when they look at objects from a distance. Descartes says that doesn't raise a general skeptical question about all of our perceptions. But why not? My experience seems to teach me the following truth: *People are often perceptually deluded.* So why doesn't that truth completely paralyze me? Since people are often perceptually deluded, how can I trust my perceptions about *when* perceptions are deluded? Maybe I am deluded about when perceptions are deluded. Evidently, it doesn't work that way. You provisionally trust your senses to build up the most specific theory you can about the nature and scope of a delusional circumstance. Only after you do that do you worry about whether some experience is vulnerable to that delusion. Or take the example of the eye drops. Since you have evidence that the drops cause non-veridical experiences, maybe they cause total hallucinations and they caused you to hallucinate that you were told they can only affect color vision. Here again the answer must be that at the first step we must trust our experience to tell us what the nature and scope is of a kind of delusion. And that's just how it is with regard to dreams. We can trust our experience that indicates that dreams are not lucid. And therefore when our experience is lucid we have no reason to worry that we are dreaming. When we are lucid we have no reason to worry that we are dreaming in just the way that, when we are close to objects, or when we have not taken the drops, we have no reason to worry that we are deluded as we might be if we are far away from objects or have taken the drops.

In all of these examples, we must at the first step allow ourselves to appeal to all of our experiences in determining the nature and scope of a delusional circumstance, prior to restricting ourselves at the second step to trusting only experiences that are not vulnerable to the delusional circumstance.

Daniel   Maybe I begin to get this. I don't know. Let me ask a question. Suppose Vatol's experience seems to indicate that the vat-people all went out of existence a minute ago as a result, let's suppose, of a change in some electromagnetic field. So that's the theory Vatol's first step arrives at. Surely that ought not to remove his reasons to doubt. But, since the proposition "My current experience is not an experience of a minute ago" is presumably not the content of an experience that is vulnerable to any relevant delusional circumstance, it seems that at the second step he can now argue, "My current experience is not vulnerable to the vat-delusional-circumstance because my current experience is not an experience of a minute ago." That's obviously absurd: his reason for doubting is surely not removed the minute he comes to believe that the vat-people have just gone out of existence.

Yitzhak   Of course that's right, and it's a good point. You might also have made the point in terms of the relevantly invulnerable judgment "I am not someone other than myself," which might prove to Vatol that he is not a vat-person, if his theory of the vat-delusional-circumstance could be said to include the fact that the vat-people are people other than himself. But the answer is that one's theory of the nature and scope of a delusional circumstance must be couched in general terms; it cannot include token-reflexive components like indexicals, tenses, or demonstratives. This seems a natural constraint that blocks various absurd results. Admittedly there are serious problems about latent indexicals and demonstratives in certain general terms, according to Kripke and Putnam, but I'll assume for our present purposes that we don't need to worry about that.

Daniel   Would it matter if we hold the A-theory, in which case tenses won't be treated in the same way as indexicals or demonstratives?

Yitzhak   *Oy vey*. Let's assume that's not going to matter here. I don't want to get involved with that.

Daniel   Okay, maybe that works. But let me give you another example. Suppose that the evidence Vatol has of the existence of vat-people includes evidence that, for deep reasons of computer technology and neurology, the vat-people hear a peculiar whistling sound every four minutes. Ordinary people do not experience any such sounds. This is part of Vatols first-step theory of the vat-delusive-circumstance. It seems to follow, on your account, that Vatol's situation vis-à-vis the vat-people is analogous to our situation vis-à-vis dreaming. Vatol can rightly determine that he is not a vat-person by appealing to the non-vulnerable fact that he does not hear that whistling sound. Can that be right? He is not allowed to appeal to the fact that he is walking down the street, to show that he is not a vat-person, but he can appeal to the fact that vat-people hear this sound, a fact that he found out, let's suppose, by walking over to the library and reading up on vat-people.

Yitzhak   Yes, I think that is right. It is, as you say, just like the dreaming issue—in fact, the issue is even clearer here, since there is no worry that vat-people might be deluded about their mental states. At the first step Vatol determines that the nature of the vat-delusive circumstance implies a certain phenomenological difference between vat-people and normal people. At the second step, he can appeal to that difference to show that he is not a vat-person. He cannot appeal at the second step to the fact that he is walking down the street because, if he were a vat-person, he could be deluded about that fact. He can appeal to the fact that he is not hearing a certain kind of sound every few minutes because, as we're supposing, even if he were a vat-person, he would not be deluded about that kind of phenomenological fact. Here is the basic point: You must be able to appeal provisionally to your best general theory of the nature of a delusional circumstance. But, given the general theory of the nature and scope of the delusion, you must not appeal to any facts that are vulnerable to the delusion in trying to show that you are not deluded. You can't appeal to the fact that you went to a library, which would show that you're not a vat-person. Or to the fact that your brain is too big to be envatted. That's the way it has to work, I think. Otherwise there can't be any coherent way of deciding on the basis of our perceptual experience that some kinds of experiences can't be trusted.

Daniel   Okay. I don't know. It's pretty complicated, the two steps and all. I don't know.

Lev   It is, *azoy vee mir zugt*, "quite a mouthful."

Yitzhak   Well, I'm afraid that may be the best I can do at the moment.

Lev Yitzhak. If I may ask a question or two.

Yitzhak Go ahead.

Lev Let us imagine that until he is forty Vatol worries about lacking a reason to believe that he is not a vat-person. Then, when he hits upon forty years, it is announced in the Jewish Daily Forward, and many lesser papers, that scientists have now discovered that the vat-people hear the whistling sound. Then Vatol says to himself, "What a big relief!" Yes?

Yitzhak Yes, that's what follows from my account. Once he learns about the whistling sound he no longer has reason to question whether he is a vat-person. It has to be understood that what I'm calling the "first step" and the "second step" is not a matter of temporal chronology; it's a matter of levels of epistemic deliberation. At any point in one's life one exercises the first step by provisionally taking into account and trusting all of one's experiences in constructing a theory of the nature and scope of delusive circumstances. When Vatol reads about the whistling factor his theory of the vat-delusive-circumstance changes, and he no longer has reason to question whether he is vat-person. One should not say that, since he determined when he was thirty that he had reason to doubt the veracity of his experience of going to the library and reading things, he must now have reason to doubt the newly acquired information about the whistling factor. No, the "first step" can occur at any point in your life, and if you have new experiences that, if trusted, would alter your theory of the nature and scope of a delusional circumstance, then you are permitted to trust those experiences, the experiences of reading something, say, even if those experiences would have been vulnerable to the delusional circumstance on the previous theory.

Incidentally, Lev's variation of the vat-example brings us back to your first question earlier, Danny, which I postponed answering. You considered a case in which your initial evidence indicated that the Matrix was a real phenomenon; only later your evidence is that it was just in a movie. At that point you have no reason to doubt because your new "first step" provides you with evidence that there is no delusional circumstance at all—one might say that your best current theory of the nature and scope of this would-be delusional circumstance is that its nature is non-existence and its scope is zero.

Lev   A stunning answer, Yitzhak! I will venture one more question, if I may. Suppose that when Vatol learns that the vat-people hear the sound he also learns that the vat-people, on the basis of their experience, believe that, while they are normal people, there are vat-people, and they believe further that only the normal people hear the sound, not the vat-people. This reassures them that they are not vat-people. When Vatol finds out all of this, he still says, "Ah, what a relief!" Yes?

Daniel   This is like your earlier example of our finding out that a billion years ago the vat-people went out of existence, but while they existed they believed that a billion years prior to them, there were vat-people who went out of existence.

Lev   Yes, it is like that.

Daniel   And your point here again is that we are uncovering differences in the salience of reasons to doubt, not differences in the reasons to doubt.

Lev Yes.

Yitzhak Well, I don't agree. I'll stick to my account if that's the best explanation I can give of why Vatol has reason to doubt and we don't.

Lev I must ask you, Yitzhak: Do all of those philosophic, legalistic convolutions and convulsions, that entire *danse macabre*, make you feel that you have reason to believe in an external reality?

Yitzhak Look. I start out with the Moorean confidence that there is an external reality, that I have reason to believe in such a reality, that I know there is such a reality. That confidence doesn't ride on my "philosophic convolutions." The philosophical task is to try to explain what is involved in our having reason for this belief. That's what I've tried to do. I admit that I can't see my way through all of the tangles here, but that's not going to affect my confidence.

Lev And Vatol will perhaps say the same thing? Vatol too will proclaim his Moorean confidence?

Yitzhak Vatol. Vatol. You know, your obsession with Vatol is really beginning to creep me out a bit. I'm not Vatol. I am not a vat-person. I am not a crook. You're no Jack Kennedy.

Daniel To be fair, Yitzhak, Lev's challenge from the start was for us to explain what the relevant difference is between us and Vatol with respect to having reason to doubt. Do you think that challenge has been met?

Yitzhak Vatol's situation seems different. I've tried to explain why, but Lev isn't convinced. And I admit that there are definitely problems left over in my explanation. By the way, something else has to be said here. Danny and I committed ourselves to the position that Vatol has reason to doubt. Probably many philosophers would question that.

Lev   Yes? Some philosophers would say that when they project themselves into Vatol's situation they do not feel anxious? Perhaps Williamson will say that all is cool because the "bad case" casts no cloud over the "good case"?[20] This is what he will say when he gets off the phone with his brother?

Yitzhak   Look, I'm not here to speak about Timothy Williamson's anxiety states. Don't ask me about that. Ask me if Williamson would say that Vatol has reason to doubt external reality.

Lev   Would Williamson say that Vatol has reason to doubt external reality?

Yitzhak   Ask me again.

Lev   Would Williamson say that Vatol has reason to doubt external reality?

Yitzhak   I think he might well say that Vatol has knowledge of external reality and has no reason to doubt.

Daniel   Really? You think Williamson might actually say that?

Yitzhak   I don't know. I think that's where his argument about the "bad case" and the "good case" might lead him.

Daniel   Okay, let's put that aside. I take it we're still committed to saying that Vatol does have reason to doubt. I frankly can't imagine denying that. So I'm afraid, Yitzhak, it's time to return to the question that has been hanging over all of this: What do we say if we have evidence that vat-people existed up to some time in the remote past, or that they will come into existence in the remote future? I mean without any evidence of a phenomenological difference.

Yitzhak   On my account this will put me in the same epistemic position as Vatol. As I said, one's theory of the existence of delusional circumstances has to be couched in non-token-reflexive terms. If I have evidence that there exist vat-people somewhere in space-time, then that gives me reason to question whether I am a vat-person. My best theory might indeed say that the vat-people went out of existence prior to the evolution of dinosaurs, but, then, any experience that might reveal that I exist after the evolution of dinosaurs is vulnerable to the vat-delusive-circumstance. So I would have entered a loop that renders all of my experience of external reality untrustworthy. But my answer to this has to be that, as things stand, I have no evidence that there ever have been or ever will be vat-people.

Daniel   Why not? Why don't you have evidence that there will be vat-people in the future? That kind of scenario is widely popular in science fiction, as in *The Matrix*. Given how technology advances, and how crazy people are, it doesn't seem at all far-fetched that at some future time vat-people will be created for some reason.

Yitzhak   Yeah, I keep saying I don't want to get involved in issues of probability, but maybe that really can't be avoided. My account says that if you have evidence that there is a certain delusional-circumstance then you can't appeal to the presumptive veridicality of experiences that are vulnerable to that circumstance. Well, how much evidence is required for the presumption of veridicality to be canceled? Maybe there is some notion here of "significant evidence." And maybe there just isn't at present significant evidence that I'm in a vat-delusional-circumstance. I don't know.

Lev   Perhaps it is a *sfek sfekah*?* First there is a *safek* whether there will be any attempt to create vat-people, and, even if there is the attempt, there is the further *safek* whether the attempt will succeed.

Daniel   Might the doubt on top of a doubt make the evidence less significant?

Yitzhak   I don't know. I don't really think that has anything to do with it.

Lev   Yitzhak. Suppose your evidence says that there is just one vat-person in the universe.

Yitzhak   Would that make the evidence insignificant? Maybe.

Lev   Suppose that one vat-person is your brother whom you spoke to on the phone.

Yitzhak   Yeah, yeah, you keep pushing for the same point, that it's just a matter of the salience of reasons that are always there. But I'm not going that route. I don't buy that. But I admit there are serious snags here that I don't know how to straighten out.

---

* In the Talmud a *safek* is a doubt; a *sfek sfeka* is, roughly, a doubt within a doubt, which may lead to a more lenient verdict than in the case of a simple doubt. See, e.g., Kesuvos 9a.

Interlude: finding an "eitzah"

Lev What you need, Yitzhak, is an *eitzah*, a Yiddish word not so easy to translate, perhaps an "escape." In Hebrew the word means advice.

Daniel Advice, a form of help. The related sense in Yiddish is an expedient, a way out. It's important in philosophy to be able to finesse an unsolved problem in one's work, to put it aside in some respectable way, so that one can move on.

Yitzhak "For present purposes I put aside the obvious and decisive refutations of my view."

Lev Yes, yes. In philosophy as in Gemara and as in life it is most essential to be able to find an *eitzah*. My brother once told me that a friend of his in Israel was thought by all to be the best boy in Yeshiva, but he had one deficit. He could not accept an *eitzah*. He searched always for a perfect *sevara*, a perfect explanation, and would settle for nothing else. The result was that he stagnated, did not *shteig* [develop], others less brilliant passed him by.

Yitzhak You know what? There should be a game show called "Find An Eitzah!" People would be given scenarios in which someone is in a tough spot and needs an *eitzah*. I'll give you an example, okay? There was this guy who got a rabbinical degree, but like the three of us, he had no interest in going into the rabbinate. But he did have a part-time job as the *mashgiach* in a kosher catering place in Long Island. You know, he had to supervise the kitchen to make sure the rules of *kashrut* were being followed. It was a very nice little job that also gave him the use of this terrific little apartment upstairs with a nice bedroom and a big parlor. Now what happened to this guy is that he went through a period of apostasy. He stopped doing anything. He kept it a secret even from his best friends. You know, he was ashamed. Part of it was that he held on to the *mashgiach* job. He didn't want to give it up.

Let me get to the *eitzah* part. When this guy gave up being *frum* one thing he loved to do was shave with a regular razor rather than with an electric razor. Obviously he had never been able to do this before, and he loved putting on a lot of shaving cream and running the razor over his face. Well, on this one occasion he's due down in the kitchen in about ten minutes and he's in the bathroom preparing to shave. He's got shaving cream all over his face. Before he starts he steps out into the parlor to get something. He must have left the parlor door ajar, because suddenly the caterer sticks his head in, sees the *mashgiach* standing there evidently preparing to shave with a razor, something that even moderately observant orthodox Jews would never dream of doing. The caterer mumbles something and withdraws in horror. So our hero is standing there in the parlor with shaving cream all over his face, due down in the kitchen in a few minutes. It's not just his job that's in jeopardy but his reputation. What can he do? Can either of you: *find an eitzah*?

Lev   Tell us the *eitzah*, Yitzhak. It is beyond my deviousness.

Yitzhak   Okay. The guy puts on his suit and tie, and a few minutes later appears in the kitchen with shaving cream all over his face— and announces that he has a rare skin disease on his face that requires shaving cream to be put on it several times a day. Can you picture this? The rabbi standing in the kitchen, with suit and tie, supervising the *kashruth*, with shaving cream all over his face! Of course there was nothing to fault him for, it's not illicit to put shaving cream on your face, he just received everyone's sympathy.

Lev A wonderful genius stroke of an *eitzah*, Yitzhak!

Daniel Okay, can we get back to where we were?

Yitzhak This concludes today's segment of: "Find an Eitzah!"

Summary

Daniel Okay, good, good. Then let me try to recapitulate this part of our discussion. We assumed that . . .

Yitzhak Give us the *essentials*, Danny!

Daniel We assumed that Vatol has reason . . .

Yitzhak The *essentials*, Danny! The *etzem zach*!

Daniel We assumed . . .

Yitzhak The *fundamentals*!

Daniel We assumed that Vatol has reason to doubt external reality. The question was whether our normal situation is epistemically better than Vatol's. Lev says no, and Yitzhak says yes. Initially, Yitzhak agreed with Lev that our actual situation is not better than if we found out that there are vat-people in the remote past or remote future: as we have no reason to doubt in our actual situation we would have no reason to doubt in that hypothetical situation. But Lev's n-to-n+1 argument made him provisionally concede that it does not matter at which point in time (or, for that matter, in space) the vat-people are believed to exist. So if it is believed that vat-people exist at any time, then there is reason to doubt. An attempt to avoid this result by appealing to a safety condition on belief seemed to fail.

In an attempt to clarify the issue, we turned to Jim Pryor's principle, which says that when you have an experience that seems to say that p, this provides you with a defeasible presumption that p is the case. The question, then, is why Vatol cannot appeal to this principle and thereby trust his experience. Yitzhak attempted to formulate rules of defeasibility that would explain why Vatol has reason to doubt but we do not. A basic distinction is between one-level and two-level cases. In two-level cases our experience provides us with evidence that there actually exists in the world a delusional-circumstance, a circumstance that actually leads people to have non-veridical perceptions. One of Yitzhak's defeasibility rules is the non-circularity constraint, which says that, if an experience is vulnerable to a certain delusional circumstance, you cannot appeal to that experience to show that you are not in that circumstance. It seems that at least in some critical examples Pryor himself does not accept the non-circularity rule. A second defeasibility rule suggested by Yitzhak says that when you enter a loop, whereby the experience that is evidence that there exists a delusional circumstance is itself vulnerable to that circumstance, then you must go *le-chumra* and distrust every experience that is vulnerable to that circumstance, including the experience that tells you of that circumstance.

And, finally, there is the very difficult idea of the two steps, which is supposed to explain why our relationship to dreaming does not provide the same reasons for doubt that are provided to Vatol by the hallucinations of the vat-people. In the first step we are permitted to ignore circularity concerns and construct our best empirical theory as to the nature and scope of a delusional circumstance. Only then, in the second step, do concerns enter about trusting vulnerable experiences. The theory constructed in the first step must be couched in general terms, and one consequence of this is that the conclusion of the n-to-n+1 argument is vindicated: reason to doubt arises no matter at which point in time or space the vat-people are believed to exist

I think that sums it up.

Yitzhak   That's it. That's all she wrote.

Three additional questions

Daniel   But I actually want to bring up a couple of other questions, which I suspect are peripheral to our main issue. The first is this. If Vatol trusts his experience, he has to distrust the experiences of other people. Is this related to the problem of disagreement with one's epistemic peers?[21] The problem there is why I'm justified in believing various philosophical or ethical propositions that my peers reject. If I'm Vatol, am I faced with that same problem? Why should I trust my perceptions when they conflict with my brother's perceptions?

Yitzhak   Are you repeating the mistake I initially made? In the standard case the question is why I should respect my own judgments more than my peers. But if I'm Vatol and I wind up doubting my experience, then I'm left with no beliefs about the existence of my brother or any other people. I can't very well say, "Out of respect for my brother I will doubt that he exists."

Daniel   That may not be the way to put it, Yitz. If I'm Vatol, either I believe that my experiences are superior to my brother's or I do not believe this. It's true that if I do not believe it, I also do not believe that there is any such person as my brother. But the option of believing it may be ruled out by the same considerations that give rise to the standard problem of disagreeing with one's peers.

Yitzhak   So you want to suggest that in examples like Vatol there is a dimension of the problem that doesn't arise in an example where there are no other people that one has to disagree with if one trusts one's experience.

Daniel   Maybe. But I certainly acknowledge that the Vatol example can't be viewed quite like the standard examples of the problem of disagreement.

Yitzhak   I think that the problem of trusting or doubting one's sense experience occurs at a more basic level, and the typical dialectical moves in the standard problem of disagreement can't apply. So I don't know if it's really helpful to compare the problems.[22]

Daniel   Yes, I think that's probably right. The comparison may not be helpful. But there is a related question. You've been assuming, Yitz, in line with the views of many philosophers, that there is an irreducible a priori principle that accords a presumption in favor of the veridicality of one's sense experience. My question, now, is whether this presumption also applies to other people's sense experience. A distinction can be made here that is analogous to the distinction in moral philosophy between agent-relative principles and agent-neutral principles.[23] An agent-relative perceptual principle will imply: Each person has an a priori prima-facie reason to believe that her own experience is veridical. An agent-neutral principle will imply: Each person has an a priori prima-facie reason to believe that any person's experience is veridical.

Yitzhak   I think it's pretty clear that in Pryor, and probably in most philosophers, it's the agent-relative principle that operates. I start out having this special a priori reason for trusting my own experience, on the basis of which I build up a picture of the world within which I may or may not trust other people's experience. How else could it work? My beliefs about what other people experience must be based on my own experience.

Lev   If I may inject a third question. I am wondering, Yitzhak, how you will answer to an argument that had been communicated to me by Miriam Schoenfield. She summons a principle of probability that maintains that A can raise the probability of B only if B raises the probability of A. That is correct, yes?

Yitzhak   That's a Bayesian principle. It says, more carefully put, that the probability of A, given B, can be greater than the probability of A, given not-B, only if the probability of B, given A, is greater than the probability of B, given not-A. I think I see where this may be going, but let's hear it.

Lev   Miriam Schoenfield conjectures that the fact that you are a vat-person or that you are always hallucinating cannot raise the probability that you will seem to experience a world containing vat-people. It then follows from the just mentioned principle that the fact that you seem to experience a world containing vat-people cannot raise the probability that you are always hallucinating.

Daniel   Ah, that is interesting! It does seem arguable that it is not a priori more probable that there should exist someone with Vatol's experiences who is hallucinating than that there should exist someone with those experiences who is not hallucinating. Either way, the occurrence of such experiences seems exceedingly improbable, and arguably equally improbable. If this is so, the probability of Vatol's having such experiences, conditional on his hallucinating, is not greater than the probability of his having such experiences, conditional on his not hallucinating. It then follows from that Bayesian principle that the probability that Vatol is hallucinating, conditional on his having such experiences, is not higher than the probability that he is hallucinating, conditional on his not having such experiences. This entails that Vatol's epistemic situation is no different from ours. The fact that he seems to experience a world containing vat-people does not make it more probable that he is hallucinating than that we are.

What do you say to that, Yitz?

Yitzhak   Is this supposed to be an argument in favor of Lev's position, that both Vatol and we have reason to doubt? It may instead be an argument in favor of the view that neither Vatol nor we have reason to doubt.

Lev   It is possible that Miriam Schoenfield would enjoy such an interpretation of her argument. But you have given us your word, Yitzhak, that you would not renege on your commitment that Vatol has reason to doubt.

Daniel   That's right, Yitz. If Schoenfield's argument is correct, we would have to take it to support Lev's view.

Yitzhak   Okay. But I reject the argument. I've repeatedly said that in claiming that Vatol has reason to doubt, whereas we don't, I'm appealing to a framework of irreducible perceptual principles rather than to any general probabilistic framework. There is an irreducible presumption in favor of trusting our experience, and this presumption goes together with irreducible defeating principles, one of which is that we go *le-chumra* in a loop. Therefore, Schonfield's Bayesian probabilistic framework doesn't provide the intuitions that are relevant here. I have no intuitive idea what probability Vatol ought to assign to the proposition that he is hallucinating. That may depend on various facts about his overall experience. That's not the issue. And, actually, I'm not sure what probability *we* ought to assign to the proposition that we are *not* hallucinating. I've expressed misgivings earlier as to whether the rational certainty—the rational outright belief—of a proposition is properly represented by an assignment of the value 1 to the probability of the proposition. I don't know about that. But we're not dealing with probability assignments. We are dealing with the difference between doubting and not doubting, between judging, "It may be that I'm just hallucinating" and not judging that. And the point is that Vatol's experience of entering a loop rationally requires him to make that doubting judgment, whereas our experience of not entering a loop requires us to not make any such doubting judgment. Of course, if we want, we can at the end of the day assign some probabilities to various propositions in Vatol's context and ours, and we can work it out so that these assignments conform to Bayesian principles, but the intuitions we appeal to in these assignments must respect the irreducible epistemic principles.

Lev   Yitzhak, these presumptions and defeatings that you love so much: you create these *ex nihilo*?

Yitzhak   No, I don't create them *ex nihilo*! We arrive at epistemic principles by considering what we say intuitively about particular examples. It seems intuitively clear to most sane people that, given our experiences, we have no reason to doubt external reality. And it also seems intuitively clear, I think, that, given Vatol's experiences, he *does* have reason to doubt. The epistemic principles I've sketched are designed to account for those intuitive reactions.

Lev's disagreement with Yitzhak

Daniel   Good, good. Perhaps Schoenfield's argument can be left for the time being. But let's not forget that Yitzhak is still faced with the question whether he really has no evidence that there will be vat-people in the future.

Yitzhak That's right. But let's be clear about something. Lev is not basing his position on the strength of that question. Lev is saying, like Descartes, that even if there was no empirical evidence of the actual existence of any delusional circumstance, a reason to doubt external reality is given by the mere possibility of perceptual delusion.

Daniel Yes, I think that's right. Vatol believes that he is surrounded by actual vat-people. We believe that we are surrounded by possible vat-people. Lev sees no difference between these cases.

Lev That is correct. The basic point is that there is no reason to believe that our sense-experience is veridical.

Daniel No reason? So you don't accept that there is any kind of special presumption in favor of the veridicality of our perceptual experience?

Lev A "special presumption"? Does the impossibility of doubt make a "special presumption"? But I am saying that there is no *reason* to trust our sense-experience. I am assuming that the necessity to believe does not mean that there is a reason to believe. It is as Hume said: our nature *overcomes* our reason. It does not *give* us a reason.

Yitzhak Well, I guess the idea is that it doesn't give us an *epistemic* reason. As we said earlier, even Vatol obviously has *pragmatic* reasons to believe. Our question is whether we have a kind of reason that, as we agree, he lacks. I think yes, and Lev thinks no.

Daniel But I think I may be losing my grip on what it means to have a reason to believe in the relevant sense. I understand that Vatol lacks a kind of reason that we may possess. But I'm beginning to feel a little lost about what that can mean.

Lev   It is surely a difficult matter. But if I may be permitted for the moment to personify Reason, as Hume often does. Reason is the intellectual faculty. And Reason is the last word, as Thomas Nagel says.[24] I would say it is the last word in the matter of having reasons, in the having-reasons department, as the Brits might say. Yes? We are in possession of epistemic reason for a belief—I am talking of all-things-considered epistemic reason for an outright belief—if Reason offers its endorsement to the belief. *Ich mein,* if it is the belief that *p*, then Reason says, "Yes, *p*." If Reason is merely saying, "It is advantageous to believe that *p*," then that is only a pragmatic reason for the belief. And if Reason only is saying, "It is not possible to doubt that *p*," then that too is not yet an epistemic reason. We have an epistemic reason only when Reason goes to saying, "*p*. Yes, *p*." Our intellect must accede to the proposition that *p*, not merely to the proposition that it is advantageous or necessary to believe that *p*. Yes?

Now Reason *forms* certain beliefs. Reason forms a priori beliefs, of logic, mathematics, metaphysics, semantics, perhaps more. Logic may include inductive logic too, the logic of probabilities. Here I certainly wish to depart from Hume. That Reason offers its endorsement to the beliefs that it itself forms does not seem immediately a big problem. Please do not misunderstand. At another level Reason may question its own veridicality, but not at the first stage.

Daniel   Miguel De Unamuno said that reason devours itself.[25]

Lev   Perhaps. Eventually. But this is a later story.

Daniel Then the lights go out completely.

Yitzhak "Put out the light, and then put out the light."[26] But, then again, we don't want anyone going by mistake in the sink here.

Lev At the first stage Reason endorses the beliefs it forms. But Reason also must offer its endorsement to beliefs that it does not form. Reason does not form introspective beliefs. But it is compelled to endorse introspective beliefs because it forms the belief that introspective beliefs are infallible; they cannot be mistaken.

Yitzhak Modulo W.

Lev What of beliefs of memory? Why is it that in philosophy thousands of pages have been written on skepticism about perception but very little on skepticism about memory?

Daniel I think that in Stroud's book *The Significance of Philosophical Scepticism* memory is not even mentioned.

Lev Memory in the basic sense of *retaining* beliefs is wed to Reason. *Ich mein*, Reason cannot function without memory. It is therefore not absurd if Reason must endorse the deliverances of memory.[27]

Yitzhak Since Reason will not abandon its children it endorses the beliefs it forms, and since it will not abandon its spouse it endorses the beliefs of memory. And what about perceptual beliefs? I have the feeling, Lev, that you're not even going to treat perceptual beliefs as a first cousin of Reason.

Lev That Reason rests under a compulsion to trust reasoning does not seem absurd. And as remembering is an essential component of reasoning it does not seem absurd that Reason rests under a compulsion to trust memory. But it is absurd to state that Reason has a compulsion to trust the beliefs of perception. *Ich mein*, there is no such "presumptive reason." My perceptual beliefs, they are like an alien presence to my Reason. They arrive with no invitation that my Reason can recognize. They are not a part of the working of my Reason as memory is. Unlike introspective beliefs they are possibly mistaken. They are therefore like alien tissue—yes?—like alien tissue grafted onto the intellect, which Reason is driven to reject. In considering and assessing these beliefs Reason is pushed towards only one judgment: "Maybe they are all mistaken." Having reason to doubt in the case of memory or reasoning is a further issue, which perhaps we should address at another time.

Daniel Sufficient unto each day the misery thereof.

Yitzhak *Ein mearvin simcha be-simcha.**

Daniel Okay. Good, good. Perhaps we have said all that we can for now on the question whether our normal epistemic situation is different from Vatol's.

Yitzhak *Taiku?†*

Daniel The issue may be clarified further at another time. But now we should go on to the question that was left over, about the impossibility of doubt. We now want to hear your explanation of this, Lev.

---

* As on p. 7, above.

† *Taiku*: this is the word, meaning roughly "Let it stand," put at the end of a Talmudic debate that cannot be resolved.

Act III

The Impossibility of Doubt

Lev's past epistemic anxiety

Lev   Daniel and Yitzhak. Of course when I was in Berkeley I was realizing unconsciously, as everyone must, that I could not possibly doubt the reality of my life, but a time passed before I was understanding this at a conscious level. In Berkeley my entire thoughts were distorted in that manner. I am remembering myself sitting on the Berkeley Hills terrorized by my thought that I was only watching my sense data pass in front of me.

Yitzhak   [Sings] I'm sitting on the dock of the bay, watching the tide roll away.[1]

Lev   I recall that just before I left Berkeley I attended the movie Spartacus.

Yitzhak   Kirk Douglas. A yid.

Lev   At the end Spartacus is hanging from the cross, suffering in the throes of death—yes?—and watching before his eyes as the Romans are slaughtering his comrades and all of his dreams and aspirations are as nothing. And I, sitting in the audience, am thinking: But at least he does not doubt that the events of his life actually transpired.

When I returned to France from Berkeley I was facing a period of mental turmoil. There grew in me a peculiar dependence on my brother. It seemed that only in his presence did my epistemic anxiety abate. It was necessary for me to be knowing his whereabouts at all times or I became distraught. Often without his awareness I would follow him to his appointments and await anxiously his reappearance, and then clandestinely follow him to his next visit. When my thoughts became unbearable I would arrive unannounced to his home even in the middle of the night.

Yitzhak   "Thus I refute solipsism," as he kicks his brother.[2]

Lev   In France I had this wonderful diminutive flat on Rue Cujas. I could almost glimpse the Jardin du Luxembourg from my window. I stood at my window often watching the stream of visitors coming to and from the Garden. The children were so cheerful. I loved so much to see them. At night I dreamt that I was walking with a friend in the Garden. It was you, Yitzhak . . . Yes, it was you . . . And we were talking lightheartedly about philosophy, perhaps about Thompson Clarke . . . Yes, Thompson Clarke . . . And then a blackness would descend into my mind. Maybe I am just dreaming! A black panic would descend on me. Maybe this is not really happening, maybe I am just dreaming!

Yitzhak   You mean in your dream you were in a panic that maybe you were dreaming.

Lev   Yes. And I spoke to you about this, revealing my fear to you. You would, I think, try to comfort me. But I of course understood that I could not rely on you to comfort me if I was merely dreaming that we were together. Presently I would make a great effort to awake, to test if I was dreaming. And I would climb out of the dream with difficulty. I would go from my bed to the window and look down at the people there and feel greatly relieved. And then the cloud would descend on me once again. Maybe I have only dreamt that I woke up! I would again try to see if I could wake myself. And again I would with great difficulty wake up.

Daniel   Let me understand this. So you actually had not yet woken up, you dreamt that you woke up.

Lev   Yes. This would happen I do not know how many times. When I was actually awake I would still try to see if I could get myself to wake up. I would close my eyes tightly and concentrate and try as hard as I could to climb out of sleep. When this ceremony did not awaken me I felt relief, but often this did not last to negate my thought that maybe this too was part of the dream . . . Yes? . . . I tormented myself. My torment was great. This happened many times for a period of months. Finally, a certain incident occurred which for reasons unknown to me put a stop to this dreadful syndrome. I was walking one morning after these terrible dreams within dreams—in the Garden. I was tormented. Apparently my behavior alarmed two young women who were there with their babies and they contacted the police. Now here I will tell you something, Daniel and Yitzhak. When the police arrived I ran! Inexplicably, I ran, I fled from them. There ensued a chase through the Garden.

Daniel   Wait. This actually happened? This was not a dream.

Lev   Yes, this actually happened. There was a chase, the police on my heels, as I raced through the Garden.

Daniel   So they caught you.

Lev   No. I was in my youth a very speedy runner, as you may recall. And I was intimate with the area, dashing through alleyways and around corners, winding me back to my apartment. I was at the window watching the police wander around looking for me with futility. Unfortunately, a half hour later they arrived at my house and arrested me. I had just received a postcard from someone and I fathom it fell from my pocket as I ran. So I was ultimately arrested.

Yitzhak   He was up on two charges. Public displays of solipsism. And impersonating a human being. By the way, who sent you that postcard?

Lev   Muttel Finkelstein.

Daniel   What? *Muttel Finkelstein!*

Yitzhak   I believe he lives in Cleveland.

Lev   Of course my brother, the *groyser* lawyer, was able to plug the whole story up. My record is unblemished. And for some reason those terrible dreams of skepticism abated after that incident. I do not know why exactly, but the terrible dreams within dreams ceased.

Daniel   But what are you telling us, Lev. You have been insisting throughout our discussion today that it is impossible to doubt external reality. But now you describe in detail how at certain moments in your life you actually doubted whether you were awake and not dreaming.

Yitzhak   Here's what I think, Lev. You accuse other philosophers of trying to conceal from themselves the obscure "unstatable" anxiety generated by the Cartesian reflection. But it seems to me that what you try to conceal from yourself is the fact that you really have doubted external reality. Maybe you still do. You keep insisting that such doubt is impossible, but your own experience seems to belie this.

Lev   Daniel and Yitzhak, I do not know whether, while I was awake during those tormented times at Rue Cujo, I actually doubted whether I was awake. I was not in control of my mind, I was during that period *azoy vee mir zugt* "out of my mind," and I therefore do not know whether "doubt" correctly describes my state. But I bring up those terrible incidents—my reason for recounting them to you at this point in our discussion—is to show the following point: If I did doubt whether I was awake you must see that I did not doubt external reality in the sense relevant to our discussion. I did not doubt that there was such a person as Yitzhak, that we had in fact known each other and often spoken to each other—indeed about Thompson Clarke. I did not doubt the basic framework—*Ich mein,* the basic framework of my existence, the people I grew up with, the people I cared about. A person could certainly come to believe that he is henceforth completely cut off from all other persons—yes?—or that perhaps he is the last person to exist in the universe. That might be—certainly it must be for almost anyone—horrible, a terrible torment to believe such a thing. But one's relationship to the people who define one's identity continues even if contact with those people is gone, even if they themselves are gone.

Interlude: memories from Yeshiva

Yitzhak   After you left Berkeley Danny and I didn't hear much from you for over a year. The next thing you write to us saying you are learning full time in a Yeshiva in Israel. What happened? Did you have an epiphany of some sort?

Lev   Learning Torah for a Jew is as natural as barking for a dog.

Daniel   Lev! That is a ... surprising analogy.

Lev   In Wittgenstein there is the thought that each form of life, each language-game, carries with it a unique range of moods and emotions, which can be only understood well from inside that form of life. Who can describe the mood of entering the *Beis Hamedrash* in the morning, opening one's *Gemara*, and *starting*, ... perhaps even starting a new *sugyah*?* The buzz of learning, the *smell* of the *Beis Hamedrish* ... Who can describe that form of excitement and joy?

Daniel   And who can explain how these arcane legalistic wranglings are for us the most fundamental form of *worship*, of closeness to *Hashem*?

---

* A *Beis Hamedrash* is an auditorium in a Yeshiva where Talmud students are paired off with a partner and sit, often in close proximity, discussing and debating passages of the Talmud with their partners, often loudly. A *sugyah* is a topic in the Talmud.

Yitzhak You mean this holds even for someone who is a complete *ployderer* [idiot]? Even when his *sevaras* are so obscure and *krum* [illogical] that they are stinking up the *Beis Hamedrish* to the point that people are jumping out the window?

Daniel Okay, good, good. Let's continue our discussion.

Yitzhak What about you, Lev? You also think that when you learn you are close to *Hashem*? Or is God as irrelevant to learning Torah as you think it is to the problem of skepticism? I have the feeling that God's existence is for you not relevant to anything.

Lev Yitzhak, will you demand that we speak like children? Shall we perhaps embrace Prof. Plantinga's "proof of God's existence" by analogy to "the problem of other minds"?[3]

Yitzhak You're really an atheist, aren't you? Tell me the truth for once. You're an *Apikoros* [apostate], right?

Daniel I think we agreed earlier that philosophy of religion won't be our topic today.

Yitzhak Do you think that religion allows us to face the that-which-cannot-possibly-be-faced? Is that it? I won't assume that the fact that this is a contradiction is something that you would necessarily consider to be a problem.

Daniel Please! Let's try to complete our discussion ... Here is how I understand your basic position at this point, Lev. You're saying that the Cartesian reflection is a deep source—not the only source but perhaps the deepest potential source—of a peculiar kind of inarticulate bewilderment and solitariness that is necessarily hidden anxiously at the bottom of self-consciousness. I take it that, according to you, reflection on death is another source. But death is not our topic.

Lev   Yes.

Yitzhak   I'm not able to understand why these feelings must be inarticulate. To the extent that they relate to the Cartesian reflection, they should be explained in terms of extreme doubt. But "doubt is not a possibility," "doubt is not a possibility." That's Lev's litany. And the anxiety that Vatol feels, and that Lev apparently thinks everyone feels deep down, is what? But I get what Lev is really driving at. I understand.

Lev   I know you understand, Yitzhak.

Yitzhak   What I understand is that you're a moron! Your basic thesis is that the highest virtue for a person is to live one's life in perpetual bewilderment and anxiety!

Lev   Perhaps there is virtue in acknowledging a necessity. But I do not wish to have any "thesis" about virtue.

Yitzhak   What you think is that deep down, under the surface of our lives, we are all mad. That under the "language game" we are all experiencing something akin to a bad peyote trip. Maybe *you* are mad, but what do you see in the world to suggest that people experience this underlying madness?

Daniel   But you have to admit, Yitz, that the self-conscious animals on our planet often behave as if they are half-mad, murdering each other and themselves unceasingly, often because of religion or ideology.

Yitzhak   Yes, we earthlings prey with an "e" even while praying with an "a." Or maybe we should say the opposite. Remember that story about the *Chafetz Chaim*.* He was driving on a road when they came across a yid lying in the mud under a carriage fixing a wheel with his *tefillin* [phylacteries] on. The *Chafetz Chaim*'s driver said, "Look at that wicked man, he works even when he prays." And the Chafetz Chaim said, no, he prays even when he works. *Dan l'kaf zechus*: Judge them charitably.[4] So maybe we pray with an "a" even while we prey with an "e." Either way we behave as if we are mad. That's granted. But the point is that this is not a matter of *necessity*. It's not as if there is no alternative to it. It's not as if some inarticulate sense that we are "alone," and "lost," and "abandoned" necessarily leads to our being in a perpetual state of madness under the surface . . . Because of the Cartesian reflection? . . . That's ridiculous . . . And what about God Himself, who according to Lev must also struggle with the Cartesian reflection? Maybe this also leads God to madness and murder!

Lev   Do you ever read the *Chumash* [Pentateuch], Yitzhak?

Yitzhak   You're a moron! And an *Apikoros*!

Daniel   Can I try to salvage something from this discussion?

Lev   Please salvage me, Daniel.

Daniel   I regret that I brought in a question about violence and war. Lev has not said anything related to such issues. It's best that we don't get involved with that.

---

* Rabbi Yisrael Meir Kagan, (1838–1933).

Yitzhak Let's see if I've got this straight: no talk about death, no talk about God, no talk about morality, no talk about political philosophy.

Lev Soon you will be rendered inarticulate, Yitzhak.

Yitzhak Never!

Lev's first argument for the impossibility of doubt

Daniel Let's talk about the claim that "doubt is not a possibility." From your remarks a few moments ago, Lev, it seems you are claiming that there is a certain "framework" that cannot be doubted. I think you called it the basic framework of your existence. Of course that will remind us of Wittgenstein's view in *On Certainty*, about "hinge" propositions. Is your view related to Wittgenstein's?

Lev I am embarrassed by this. It seems clear that Wittgenstein holds, as I do, that certain doubts are impossible, not as a matter of contingent psychology, but as a matter of necessity. Wittgenstein says in *On Certainty* that doubting certain facts would "knock us off our feet," would make us "give up all judgment," would "plunge us into chaos" because it would take away from us "the foundation of judgment."[5] I am embarrassed to say a complaint against Wittgenstein that he seems to *intellectualize* the issue in a wrong manner.

Daniel Wittgenstein is guilty of *over intellectualizing*? That *is* a surprising complaint against him.

Lev Yes, Daniel. It surprises me and perplexes. But Wittgenstein speaks of the foundation of judgment that would be lost by certain doubts, when I think he should speak of the foundation of love.

Yitzhak Have you gone completely nuts? The foundation of *love*? What does love have to do with it?

Lev Wittgenstein seems to be carrying forth like a *Quine* who says that certain beliefs are immune from revision because to revise them would be too much havoc to the … to the, as I think he says, intellectual economy and coherence of the web of beliefs. But why would the losing of belief in external reality have to adversely affect my so-called "theory" to that degree? *Ich mein*. Why could I not be having coherent beliefs and inferences about my sense experience? The answer to this cannot be given in intellectual terms. The cognitive void that must necessarily result from a loss of one's belief in external reality, the cognitive void—yes?—would not result most primarily from the intellectual dissonance that this loss would entail, no, but from the obliteration of the entire structure of one's reasons of love, *Ich mein*, from the annihilation of any experience of meaning to one's existence.

Daniel Oh, I see! We're talking about "love" in Frankfurt's technical sense.[6]

Lev Yes. My thinking on these matters has been influenced by the work of Harry Frankfurt.

Yitzhak *Heshie?*

Daniel You're personally acquainted with Frankfurt?

Yitzhak   No, I've never met him. Have you?

Daniel   Go on, Lev.

Yitzhak   I remember now what Frankfurt says about love. But I don't like that word.

Daniel   So we've heard.

Yitzhak   I mean I think it muddies things up in this kind of discussion. I think Frankfurt says that you "care" about something if you not only desire it, but desire to desire it. And you "love" something if you care about it as an end in itself. But that seems to be a peculiar use of both the words "care" and "love." We could just talk more clearly about "reflective desire" and "reflective desire for something as an end in itself."

Lev   I am able to forswear "love" out of my love for you, Yitzhak. We can indeed talk of reflective desire.

Daniel   There is also "valuing" and "identifying." There is a tangle of closely related concepts here. But perhaps we don't need to get too deeply involved in that right now. Perhaps you can tell us what your main point is, Lev. In what sense are you saying it's impossible to doubt external reality?

Lev   Then I will give two presentations. The first will be in terms of valuing, and the second in terms of the identity of the self. They are different but related.

Daniel   Okay, good. So you are going to explain, first, how you see the notion of valuing as leading to the result that it is impossible to doubt external reality.

Yitzhak Really? Good luck with that!

Lev My argument from valuing has two premises. The first premise is that it is impossible for a being to value its life, or anything in its life, if it does not believe it has meaningfully interacted with other lives. The second premise is that it is impossible for a being to be intellectually responsible if it does not value anything in its life. From these two premises the conclusion follows that it is impossible for a being to be intellectually responsible if it does not believe that it has meaningfully interacted with other lives.

Yitzhak Wait a minute! Does that really get you the result you wanted? You said that Vatol cannot doubt. But now you're only saying that he can't doubt insofar as he is "intellectually responsible."

Lev Yes, I was assuming that Vatol was of sound mind, that he did not go insane because of his experiences. One of my main interests of course is whether intellectually responsible philosophers who delve into the Cartesian reflection might doubt external reality. My conclusion is that this is not a possibility.

Yitzhak But you're allowing that lunatics might have such doubts?

Lev Yes, in my main arguments I do allow this. I am actually inclined to think that no being, whether intellectually responsible or not, could possibly doubt external reality. But I would like to leave that for later. It is a less important position and one that I am less confident about.

Daniel Okay, let's leave that for later. But maybe we can initially try to clarify some terminology. An "intellectually responsible" being means what exactly?

Lev   An intellectually responsible being is rational in the way that persons of sound mind are rational. Such a being is committed to standards of truth and reason. Such a being exercises control over its cognition to satisfy those standards.

Yitzhak   Are you presupposing a "voluntarist" view according to which one can control what one believes?

Daniel   I don't think that's implied by what Lev just said. Although we may be unable to directly control our beliefs or doubts, we can normally exert a great degree of control over the intellectual activities that lead to belief or doubt. A being is intellectually responsible in the relevant sense only if it holds itself responsible to certain standards of intellectual control, such standards as being focused, careful, thorough, and honest in pursuing the truth.

Lev   Yes, thank you, Daniel. I do not hold that we can believe because we decide to believe. But we can decide to control our thoughts in the direction of truth and reason. This is to be intellectually responsible.

Daniel   I take it that we're not ruling out that an intellectually responsible being might on some occasions allow its beliefs to be swayed by pragmatic reasons, but it must have a general commitment to moving its thoughts in the direction of truth and reason.

Lev   Yes, that is the idea.

Daniel   In other words, even an intellectually responsible being might have some beliefs or doubts that are not guided by a commitment to truth and reason, and that are themselves in a sense *not* intellectually responsible. Indeed, our belief that our perceptual experiences are reliable in revealing an external reality may be in Vatol or, if Lev is correct, even in us a belief that is not guided by a commitment to truth and reason. But Vatol and we are intellectually responsible beings in that, once having accepted that general belief in the reliability of our experience, our subsequent beliefs and doubts are generally guided by the commitment to truth and reason.

Lev   Yes.

Yitzhak   Couldn't there be people who form beliefs in ways that are directed at truth and involve reasoning but who don't have any general commitment to moving their thoughts in the direction of truth and reason? Couldn't they be reliably responsive to evidence without being "committed" to responding to evidence? Might not such people be rational and of sound mind?

Daniel   Perhaps there could be such people, "intellectual wantons" as they might be called, where a wanton in Frankfurt's sense is a being who does not have second-level desires and evaluations directed towards its first-level states. But I'm not sure whether a being who is merely responsive to evidence without being committed to truth and reason would thereby remain focused, would not be distracted by every change of mood or context, would reason slowly enough or review its reasoning sufficiently. So I'm not sure whether such a being deserves to be called rational and of sound mind. I doubt it. One thing I think is that such a being could probably not engage in philosophical thought, and, specifically, could have no motive to reflect on whether there actually is an external reality. In any case, Lev's argument does not as yet deal with beings other than those who are in the indicated sense intellectually responsible. Certainly philosophers are intellectually responsible in that sense, and, as Lev just said, his main conclusion at present is that philosophers cannot possibly doubt external reality.

Yitzhak   Good enough. Let's go on.

Daniel   Okay, perhaps that clarifies the meaning of the second premise, which says that intellectual responsibility requires valuing aspects of one's life. The first premise requires for such valuing that the being believes it has meaningfully interacted with other lives. "Meaningful interaction" is what?

Lev   Simply interactions that are noticed by the being and that matter to it.

Daniel   Okay, maybe that's good enough. And what is this business of "other *lives*"? Do you mean other persons?

Lev   Probably it amounts to this. But perhaps there can be person-like beings that are not quite persons. I would like to leave some latitude. The formulation is at least clear in requiring a belief in external reality.

Yitzhak   Let me try to get this straight. Maybe I've already asked this question before. You're saying, Lev, that philosophers, who are presumably of sound mind, can't possibly doubt external reality. But haven't philosophers often claimed to have such doubts? What are you saying, that these philosophers are *lying*?

Daniel Yitz, let's not place that problem on Lev's lap. As we've said earlier, many philosophers have said that no philosophers have doubted external reality. Even Descartes says at one point that no person of sound mind has ever doubted external reality.[7]

Yitzhak So philosophers who claim to doubt external reality are lying?

Daniel Maybe they are confused in some way. Maybe they confuse doubting with believing that they lack knowledge, a belief that they may well have, and that Lev himself might not even reject. Or perhaps when we finally get to discuss the "two-level" view the professed doubts of these philosophers will be clarified. But let's now focus on Lev's seemingly distinctive argument for the claim that doubt is impossible.

Yitzhak Fine.

Daniel Okay. So let's now talk about whether we find the premises of the argument convincing. The second premise seems immediately plausible to me. It seems that an intellectually responsible being must at least value having beliefs that are true and that satisfy the demands of reason. What do you say, Yitz?

Yitzhak I guess I can accept the second premise for the moment, although I'm not so clear what is being packed into the word "valuing."

The first premise of Lev's first argument

Daniel Okay, so maybe we can concentrate on the first premise. Why do you claim, Lev, that a being could not value its life or aspects of its life if it does not believe that it has interacted with other lives?

Lev   To live without believing this would be to have a life of unfathomable solitude, if I may use an expression conveyed to me by Georges Dicker. I am saying in the first premise that a life of unfathomable solitude is not a possible object of valuing for the being living that life.

Yitzhak   Why not? Why can't such a life be valued? I don't know what you mean by *unfathomable*. But why can't this solitary character value sensations of pleasure, or value solving mathematical puzzles? I take it that you're not making an empirical speculation about human psychology. You're claiming these things as a matter of necessity. But isn't it at least coherently conceivable that the solitary being will value a life of pleasureful sensations and thinking about mathematics?

Lev   No, that is not conceivable!

Yitzhak   You're just announcing that?

Lev   You must emphasize in reflecting on this matter that the solitary being is not like a castaway who perhaps despairs of ever connecting again to another living being, but who well remains connected in his memories to other beings. This person may certainly value his life. A subject of euthanasia who perhaps is not valuing the *remains* of his life may yet be valuing his life as a whole, *Ich mein*, his existence. But the solitary being can find nothing in his life to be valuing. To be valuing one's life is to find meaning in it. But there is not, and cannot conceivably be, meaning in a life that is not believed by the one who lives it to be connected to other lives.

Daniel We as observers may certainly value some of the solitary being's acts because of how they affect others we care about, but the assumption, I take it, is that if the solitary being could value them, this would have to be for self-regarding reasons.

Lev Yes, and my assumption also is that the background condition for valuing anything in one's life for self-regarding reasons is that one values one's life, one's self, one's existence. And it is not conceivable that this being could value its life.

Yitzhak This stuff about the "meaning" in life is obscure. But, in any case, you're simply issuing an announcement that these things are not conceivable. Why should anyone believe it?

Daniel Let's be fair, Yitz. Philosophers often just "announce" a modal claim, such as Kripke's necessity of origins.

Yitzhak But I don't think I see any intuition here.

Daniel I think I do. To value your life is not just a matter of having a "conatus" by which you "endeavor to persist in your own being." A wanton being who has no second-level reflective consciousness may endeavor to persist in its own being, but it cannot value its life in the relevant sense. That must necessarily be the status, Lev is saying, of a solitary being who does not believe that its life is touched by other lives. Such a being may still have wanton impulses, urges, or desires in the broadest sense, but cannot be a responsible agent, and therefore cannot be rational in the sense in which intellectually responsible persons are rational. At the end of one of his papers, Frankfurt maintains that a wanton being could not reason or deliberate because it could not "decide" or "make up its mind."[8] This is closely related to Lev's claim in his second premise that a being who does not value its rational cognition cannot reason in a responsible manner.

Lev   Yitzhak, I am thinking that what will greatly help here is a certain phenomenological exercise. The modal intuition that I am expressing in the first premise cannot be appreciated from an abstract distance. One must be phenomenologically engaged. I suggest the phenomenological exercise of trying to imagine what it would be like to be such a solitary being. But you must not stand at a distance. *Ich* mein, you must not be saying, "Okay, that is easy, here I am, doubting that there are enduring and causally related substances in space." The imagining must be highly personal. In one place Norman Malcolm tries to imagine doubting that there is really an inkbottle in front of him.[9] But it is not of great personal significance whether there is really an inkbottle.

Yitzhak   Who knows what those Cornell guys were doing with their inkbottles through those long cold Ithaca winters?

Lev   Descartes endeavors to imagine in Meditation 1 doubting whether he is really there in his nightgown in front of the fire. That is still far from the personal imagining we are requiring. In this phenomenological exercise you are thinking about some of the people most attached in your life. Your children, your spouse, your friends, your colleagues, your parents, your siblings. You are picturing these people in your mind, you are recalling each one by name, *Ich mein*, picturing *concretely* and with *vividness* very important interactions which you have had with them. This must take some time to be dwelling on. The next step in the experiment is that you are endeavoring to imagine what it would be like to doubt the reality of those people and interactions. You must try to imagine what such doubts would be like for you, what it would *feel like* to have such doubts.

Yitzhak   I've already said that I think such doubts would scare the hell out of me. But you apparently want to go deeper into the "phenomenology" of this. I'm not getting involved with that. I'm not into these kind of weird head games.

Lev   Yes, I know.

Yitzhak   What do you mean, you know?

Lev   You do not like weird experiences since that peyote many years ago.

Yitzhak   So what's wrong with that?

Lev   It is not wrong. I am hoping for you that you shall have no weird experiences.

Daniel   Okay. It appears we will not at present be able to share our notes on the outcome of that phenomenological exercise. What do you think the outcome is, Lev?

Lev   One finds that one can as easily imagine what it would be like to be a bat as to imagine what it would be like to be a solitary being.

I am talking of a solitary being who, while retaining a sound mind, is lacking a belief in any interactions with other lives. *Ich mein,* we understand that it is not following from this finding that such a solitary being is impossible, any more than bats are impossible. Nevertheless, something is greatly learned from the exercise. For as you are endeavoring to approach the point of projecting yourself imaginatively into the mental state of the solitary being—yes?—you find yourself experiencing a peculiar kind of vertigo and anxiety, *Ich mein,* a sense of being engulfed by oblivion. You will enjoy more to describe what is imaginatively happening to you as the *disappearance of your consciousness, Ich mein,* to be describing it as the disappearance of your consciousness rather than as being in a state of doubting the reality of the people in your life. I am of the opinion that anyone who conducts this phenomenological experiment must have such an experience. The reason for this, I am opining, is that, in endeavoring to imagine what it would be like to be such a solitary being, you are endeavoring to imagine a state of affairs that is impossible.

Daniel   That is interesting. I should try the exercise myself at another time. But let me at the moment suggest that there are some things that can be said about the difference between desiring and valuing that might make the first premise seem more attractive. Let me make an attempt at that. Let me say first that the connection between valuing something and judging it to have value or to be good is rather tangled and obscure, but I think it is tolerably clear that the two notions are not equivalent. Valuing is in some sense *personal.* Valuing something, unlike judging it to be valuable, must normally involve desiring it. I may value the happiness of my child more than I value the happiness of someone else's child, though I may judge the latter to be as objectively valuable as the former.[10]

Now, desire in the broadest sense might be viewed as analogous to a kind of amorphous matter that can enter into the constitution of more specific attitudes—or emotions or feelings—such as valuing or being afraid. As being afraid of something must normally involve the desire to avoid it, valuing an act must normally involve the desire to do it. But more than that, it must normally involve the reflective desire to do it, the desire to desire to do it. It may also involve the desire to do it even on the condition that one loses the desire.[11] None of this is to suggest that valuing is reducible to some configuration of desires, but I think it's important in considering Lev's position to emphasize the point that valuing requires a reflective consciousness, a kind of consciousness that has attitudes towards its own states. Michael Bratman talks at one point of "reflective valuing" as an important kind of valuing.[12] I think we should assume that it is this kind of reflective valuing that figures in Lev's argument. A dog is presumably in Frankfurt's sense a wanton that does not have this kind of reflective consciousness. A dog, therefore, can have the desire, or urge, or impulse to leave the room but cannot value leaving the room. According to Lev's first premise, a solitary creature—a creature that lacks a belief in external reality—might *desire* to avoid pain or even to prove Goldbach's conjecture but cannot possibly *value* these acts.

Yitzhak But why not? Why can't he value those acts as well as desire them?

Daniel Because there are necessary constraints on what can be valued. There may be no constraints on the possible objects of desire in the broadest sense, but it seems clear that there are such constraints on the possible objects of more specific attitudes. We struggle to understand the claustrophobic's fear of being in a confined space and may be driven to assume that he perhaps unconsciously fears the walls closing in and crushing him, or fears being isolated and abandoned. We make this assumption because being in a confined space is not in itself a suitable object of fear. Or consider as another example that we could make no sense of someone who does not morally disapprove of murder, torture, rape, or dishonesty, but only disapproves of anti-Semitism. Although anti-Semitism is a perfectly suitable object of moral disapproval, it cannot possibly be the *only* object of that attitude. Whatever is going on in this subject's mind it cannot possibly be what counts as *moral disapproval*. In the same way, whatever may be going on in the solitary being's mind, that cannot count as its valuing its life.

Yitzhak And that's because a life of "unfathomable solitude" cannot possibly be an object of valuing by the solitary being?

Daniel I think so.

Lev I enjoy very much what you have said, Daniel. Alan Gibbard has commented that normal anger is directed, but there may be cases of abnormal anger that is undirected.[13] How are we telling that it is undirected? It is because we are seeing that there is no suitable object for it to be directed at. One of my sons in his teenage period would often become angry in the late afternoon. He complained that he could not understand what he was angry at. He did not answer that he was angry at the late afternoon. The object of an attitude must be suitable. But perhaps Yitzhak will never agree that the solitary being's life cannot be for that being a possible object of valuing. Perhaps my second presentation in terms of the self will please him better.

A question about valuing one's life on the basis of probabilities

Yitzhak   Let me first raise another kind of question. It's clear that Lev assumes that a vat-person can value his life and be intellectually responsible. Since in the vat-person's delusion he mistakenly believes that he has children with whom he interacts, he can value his interactions with his children, and, by the same token, he can value his interactions with various other lives, so he can value his life. Now there is a little problem here that should be cleared up. It seems that in many typical examples the word "values" functions as a "factive" verb, so that p must be true in order for someone to value that p.[14] In these examples valuing involves valuing that something is the case. Maybe there are other examples, like "valuing world peace," in which valuing doesn't involve *valuing-that*, so that the issue of factiveness doesn't arise, but it seems clear that the sense of valuing that figures in Lev's argument involves valuing that certain interactions are aspects of his life. To value certain interactions or other aspects of one's life, or to value one's life itself, means in this context to value the fact that there are those interactions or aspects, or to value the fact that one is alive. If it follows that the sense of "values" here has to be treated as a factive, we could not say that the vat-person values his interactions with his children, since there really were no such interactions. But I think the answer to this is quite straightforward. There is in this kind of context a natural non-factive use of "values" that does allow us to say that the vat-person values his interactions with his children. In this non-factive use we are only trying to describe the vat-person's subjective attitudes. This non-factive sense may be viewed as derivative of the factive sense. The vat-person would sincerely describe his subjective attitudes in the primary factive sense by saying, "I value that I have interactions with my children." Instead of our describing his subjective state by reporting on what description he would sincerely give, we allow ourselves the simpler expedient of using "values" in a derivative non-factive sense, and we say, "Although he doesn't really have any children to interact with, he believes he does, and he values that he has interactions with his children."[15] I'm sure there are a lot of complications here, but I think this is good enough for now. Notice that the derivative non-factive sense kicks in only when the relevant belief is outright. If someone only believes that it is probable that he interacts with his children, then there seems to be no sense in which he can be said to value the interactions he's had with his children. He cannot coherently say, "I value that I have interactions with my children, though it may be that there are no such interactions."

Now, besides the vat-person there are two other characters that need to be considered. First, there is a solipsist, who, I'll take it, believes—believes outright—that he does not interact with any other lives. Then there is the character we've been referring to as the solitary being, who suspends his judgment, and neither believes he does, nor believes he doesn't, interact with other lives. Let's suppose that with respect to the solipsist I grant what Lev is saying. Since the solipsist believes that he does not interact with other lives, he cannot value his life, and he therefore cannot value pleasureful sensations and doing mathematics. Let that be granted. It doesn't immediately follow that the solitary being can't value his life. Suppose a philosopher converts to skepticism about the external world when he is forty; he suspends his belief, that is, his outright belief in an external reality. At this point he turns into a solitary being. But, like many traditional skeptics, he believes that it is quite *probable* that he is in contact with an external world and that he does in fact have children with whom he interacts. He doesn't believe these things in the outright sense of belief we're employing, in the sense that precludes any kind of doubt, but he does think that these things are probable. Why can't that probability judgment be enough to let him value his life? Why can't he value his life as a life in which he is probably interacting with his children? Although it can't be said that he values his interactions with his children, because he lacks a belief in such interactions, it can be said that he values the probability of the interactions. Why can't that be enough to allow him to value his life?

Daniel   Lev had earlier raised a question about whether it makes good sense to assign probabilities in the sense of degrees of belief to there being an external world, but perhaps he would not want to have to rely on that argument at this juncture.

Yitzhak   Really my point doesn't require the solitary being to assign a high probability, or any specific probability, to the reality of the interactions. Consider the possession of a lottery ticket. One may value possessing the ticket just because there is some probability that it is a winning ticket. The solitary being can value his life because there is some probability that it is a winning life in which the interactions are real.

Daniel   One problem I see here is that he can't really interact very well with his children without believing they are real. He cannot have a subjective attitude of love towards them without believing they are real. It's hard to imagine what sort of relationship he can have with them. So perhaps, despite the probability that they are real, there is no probability that he has a relationship with them that he can value.

Yitzhak   That may well be true for his relationship with them after he is forty. But he can value the probability of his having had good and real relationships with them at earlier times. As Lev has said, you can value your life because of your past.

Daniel   Do you have any response to Yitz's objection, Lev?

Lev   I have often heard it said that one may desire or value a thing either as an end or as a means. But there is a third manner. One may value a thing because of probabilities. This need not be to value it as an end or as a means. Suppose that if I am honored with an award I would value that as an end. Then I may value the probability of winning the award. But the probability of winning an award is not a means to win an award. Nor do I value the probability as an end in itself. This is a third manner of valuing.

I have said that the solitary being cannot value pleasureful sensations or doing mathematics. But I would acquiesce that in a normal life such things could indeed be valued. In the context of a life that is valued, such things can be valued. My contention was that, since the solitary being cannot value any interactions with other lives, it cannot value its life, and therefore cannot value any activity in its life. It is evident that my contention is that all valuing is rooted in the valuing of interactions with other lives. It is the valuing of interactions that allows one to value one's life and with that to value various other things.

What I have just said about the valuing of pleasureful sensations and doing mathematics, I also say about the valuing of the probability of interactions. In a normal life that is valued, the probability of interactions can be valued. However, the solitary being cannot value the probability of interactions because it cannot value its life. It cannot value its life because it cannot value any interactions. It cannot value any interactions because it lacks a belief in them.

Yitzhak   So you just insist that all valuing must ultimately rest on the valuing of interactions. What is your argument for that claim?

Lev   Yitzhak, you are asking too many questions.

Yitzhak   In that case, I beg your forgiveness.

Lev   What is required here is a phenomenological insight. The arguments can only guide one towards that insight. But you will not allow yourself to be guided. The basic insight is into the void, the abyss, of the solitary being's perspective. The suggestion that reflective valuing or responsible reasoning could conceivably occur within that void is a phenomenological absurdity.

Yitzhak   A "phenomenological absurdity"! *Azoy*! [Really!]

Lev   Perhaps I should attempt my second presentation.

A comparison of Lev's position with Kant's and Wittgenstein's

Daniel   Before that, there is a question I have that is probably not very significant, but it is bothering me a bit. What seems to me most distinctive about your position, Lev, is that it has a certain anti-intellectualist flavor, as you yourself intimated earlier. In Kant's *Critique of Pure Reason* it is argued that understanding must be structured in a particular manner, and, at least on some interpretations, it is implied that it is impossible to doubt some such proposition as, "There is a world beyond my consciousness that contains enduring (physical) substances that causally interact with each other in space and time." Perhaps it is also implied that sense experience must be interpreted in the light of that proposition. Much is unclear in this, of course, but it seems clear that your position, Lev, is very different. Your central claim is that the propositions that cannot possibly be doubted concern a person's interactions with other persons. Well, you say "other *lives*," and that is the source of my worry, but let me put that aside for a moment. Your central claim, then, is that the facts that a person cannot possibly doubt constitute in some sense the emotional core of the person's existence, facts that in some sense give meaning to the person's life. These facts will normally include people that the person has been emotionally attached to, and events and interactions involving those people. These are the facts that, according to your claim, it is impossible to doubt. To put this a bit more carefully, you are claiming, as I understand it, that it is necessary that at any time in a person's life the person has various beliefs about his meaningful interactions with persons in the external world. Although I assume it may be possible, perhaps within limits, to replace these beliefs with other beliefs about different interactions, it is not possible to simply suspend these beliefs, replacing them with doubt, and leaving the person with no beliefs of the required sort about external reality.

A central difference between Kant's position and yours might be highlighted by considering how these positions relate to the problem of other minds. It seems that the necessary structures of understanding proposed by Kant imply nothing about other minds. The same can perhaps be said of Wittgenstein "hinge" propositions in *On Certainty*. As you said earlier, Lev, it seems unclear why a person's hinge propositions could not be solely about the person's subjective experience, and it certainly seems unclear why the hinge propositions would necessarily include other minds.

Lev   Yet I believe Wittgenstein does make it clear in the *Investigations* that he considers it impossible to doubt the reality of other minds.

Yitzhak   Because of his behaviorism.

Lev   That is nonsense. He asserts that if you try to imagine that other people have no consciousness, this will merely fill you with a feeling of uncanniness.[16]

Daniel   I don't know. I suppose that the private language argument might also bear on this. On some interpretations the argument purports to show that a necessary condition of understanding is that one belongs to a linguistic community, which may require—though I don't know if Wittgenstein thought this– that one believes that one belongs to a linguistic community. It is not clear, Lev, whether your argument might imply that one must believe that one belongs to a *community* of persons with whom one interacts in meaningful ways, but certainly the stress is not particularly on language. A fundamental underlying difference of approach is that in both Kant and Wittgenstein the primary focus seems to be on the requirements of the intellect, whereas, for you, the primary focus is on the requirements of "love," the requirements of the intellect being derivative.

Lev   Daniel, in Wittgenstein, "language," the "language game," is always associated with a broader notion of "forms of life," which may make the difference you are bringing out less definite.

Daniel   Maybe, maybe, but I think there is still a large difference of emphasis, at least if we confine ourselves to *On Certainty* and the *Investigations*. Indeed, your injection of an emotional element into the issue of skepticism is likely to bring to mind William James's discussion in "The Will to Believe,"[17] but, as I'm sure you'll agree, this is a confusion. James observed that our emotions are likely to affect our beliefs, even in science, and he held, to put it crudely, that there are contexts in which wishful thinking is reasonable. But to suggest that our belief in an external reality is a case of wishful thinking would be to miss the basic claim you're trying to defend. The claim is that a necessary condition for having a genuinely rational consciousness—a consciousness capable of responsible reasoning—is that one have an indefinite number of beliefs about one's interactions with other lives. The distinction made by James between a belief that is based on purely intellectual grounds and a belief that is wishful thinking is itself a distinction that presupposes a context in which we are able to reason responsibly, and therefore presupposes a context in which we believe in an external reality.

But now I come to what is bothering me, Lev. You explained earlier that you don't want to simply say that we must value interactions with *persons*, because you want to leave some leeway. Perhaps it would be enough to interact with some "person-like" being, you said. But how much latitude are you allowing here? Might it turn out at the end that you are not really requiring anything beyond a belief in some structured external reality, as perhaps in Kant? I realize that, for the reasons you explained, you are not talking about castaways, but there is an interesting example in that movie with Tom Hanks in which he plays a man marooned alone on an island for a number of years. He has a volleyball on which he draws a face, and he gives it a name and talks to it. When it is eventually lost he mourns it as if it were a person.

Yitzhak Are you asking whether this might be enough to satisfy Lev's condition? I don't see that as a serious problem, Danny. There will be borderline cases. There are borderline cases in everything. I don't think that's a problem. But I'm not sure that the example you mention even qualifies as a borderline case. I would suppose that Lev's condition requires the belief that one is interacting with another *mind*, a notion we just recently mentioned. There may well be a margin of vagueness in the notion of a mind, but it's clear-cut that a volleyball does not have a mind. Of course if one suffers from the delusion that it does have a mind, then that may do the trick in satisfying Lev's condition, but the contrast with someone like Kant remains clear, since Kant apparently had no requirement to believe in other minds.

Lev   I agree with all that Yitzhak has now said. There will always be borderline cases. Not just in what is meant by a "life" or a "mind," if that word were used instead, but in what is meant by an "interaction." There is a scene in *Waiting for Godot*, probably I do not remember this with accuracy, but I will give my impression. One man says to the other, "I want to ask you a question," and the other man says, "Excellent! Let us do that. You ask me a question, then I will ask you a question. Then you will ask me a question. We can pass the time." A peculiar language-game! Even parallel play may be an "interaction." Certainly I cannot resolve what exactly will count as "interacting with another life."

Daniel   Rav Aharon says in one place that in matters of degree, matters of *shiur*, where it's a question of what exact measure is required, it must be *kiblu chazal*, that is, a judgment transmitted by God through the prophets.[18]

Lev   I am afraid it is unlikely that prophetic energy will be expended on the issue we are discussing as to the exact requirements for an interaction with other lives.

Yitzhak   We should be discussing the exact measures required for *tefillin*. That might earn a prophetic intervention.

Daniel But before we turn to *tefillin*, let us hear Lev's second argument.

Interlude: Yitzhak's tale

Yitzhak Wait a minute. I've got a story. There was this guy who was an observant Jew into his 30s. Then he gave it up.

Lev He is perhaps the same as the earlier shaving cream genius?

Yitzhak Could be . . . Anyway he got married, had a family. Years passed. But he kept having these old Shlomo Carlebach tunes running through his head. He started humming and singing them around the house. His wife couldn't stand it. [Sings] *Ko-ol penu elai, ko-ol penu elai.*

Daniel "A voice: turn to me"*

Yitzhak His wife couldn't stand it.

Lev His pitchiness?

Yitzhak That was probably it. Anyway, you know, this guy had not put on *tefillin* for over ten years. One day the thought occurred to him: Can I still do it? Do I still remember how? So he decided to try it once. You can't blame him. He had these two hypotheses, these two theories, you know: It could be done or it couldn't be done. Obviously he had to test it.

---

* Hoshana Rabbah prayer, adapted from Isaiah 45.22

Lev   He had funding?

Yitzhak   Not yet, it was just a preliminary study. Of course it turned out he was able to do it. The memory was in his bones. In his fingers.

Lev   In his finger bones.

Yitzhak   So he started to do it every day. They had this closet with the kids' games in it, and he would scrunch in there every morning and *leg tefillin*. Of course his wife found out. Obviously he knew she would. She couldn't forgive him.

Daniel   She was persecuting him.

Yitzhak   No, no, she had nothing against it. It was just that she couldn't understand him anymore. She couldn't see him that way. She said that he had removed himself from her.

Lev   He *had* removed himself from her. She did not command that he hide in a closet. With the kids' games. What was he hiding from? He thought that she did not want to see him that way? Or he did not want to see her as someone who saw him that way.

Yitzhak   Maybe he thought that she did not want to see him as someone who saw her as someone who saw him that way.

Lev   More plausible, yet.

Yitzhak   That's what killed them. Too many iterations. I think that's what Nagel says in his paper on sexual perversion. More than two iterations destroy the moment. Or was it less than two?

Daniel   Can we please get back to what we were talking about and try to finish this up? Lev, let us hear your second argument.

Lev's second argument

Lev In this argument there are three premises. The first premise says that it is impossible for a being to have any degree of self-esteem if the being does not believe that it has meaningfully interacted with other lives. The second premise says that it is impossible for a being to have a self if the being has no degree of self-esteem. The third premise says that it is impossible for a being to be intellectually responsible if it does not have a self. From these three premises the conclusion follows that it is impossible for a being to be intellectually responsible if it does not believe that it has meaningfully interacted with other lives.

Daniel The solitary being will have "no degree of self-esteem." That's a somewhat odd formulation.

Lev If I were to say that the solitary being must have "no self-esteem" you might take me to mean that such a being must have very *low* self-esteem. But what I mean is that the solitary being has no self-esteem in the way that a dog has no self-esteem. It makes no sense to talk of self-esteem with regard to the solitary being. And I therefore continue in the second premise to say that the solitary being does not have a self, in the way that a dog does not have a self. A dog has no self, it has no sense of self-identity; the same for the solitary being. And the final premise says that if a being has no self, in the way that a dog has no self, then this being cannot be a responsible cognitive agent. It cannot be a responsible cognitive agent in the way that rational persons are responsible cognitive agents. The solitary being, having no self, cannot responsibly direct its intellectual activities in pursuit of truth and reason.

Yitzhak   Now, that *is* a mouthful. And your English has suddenly become suspiciously a lot better!

Daniel   I predicted it would improve as our conversation progressed.

Yitzhak   But, Lev, can you explain, pray tell, why it makes no sense to talk of the solitary being's self-esteem?

Lev   I am of the opinion that it is built into the concept of self-esteem that one's degree of self-esteem depends on the degree to which one believes oneself to compare favorably to certain other beings. It is therefore a conceptual necessity that one's self-esteem is dependent on how one ranks oneself relative to other comparable beings that one believes to really exist.

Daniel   There may be some connection between what you are saying and some of Hume's ideas about pride at the beginning of Book 2 of the *Treatise*, but actually I think that probably goes off in a quite different direction.[19] So let's leave Hume's exegesis aside. Also, Sartre's idea of "the look" seems relevant.[20] But let's just focus on your formulation, Lev. You talk of self-esteem. Would you say the same for self-worth, self-respect, perhaps self-image? These notions too cannot apply to the solitary being?

Lev   Yes, yes! We will return to these matters. But my first premise begins with a statement about self-esteem, which is the easiest, in my opinion. There is of course a connection to what I claimed about valuing in the first argument, but now I am not assuming, what Yitzhak challenged, that valuing must begin with valuing interactions. My focus in this second argument is on the conditions for having a self.

Daniel I take it that feelings of shame and pride are normally one important kind of index of one's degree of self-esteem. I agree that it seems nonsensical to imagine someone who, while knowing that Superman is only a fiction, feels ashamed of being weaker than Superman, or feels proud of having bested people in his dreams. In these kinds of examples, it does seem rather clear that pride or shame depends on comparing oneself to people that one believes are real. But can't one feel proud of the extent to which one "lives up to one's own standards"? That looks like an example of gaining self-esteem that has no dependence on belief in other people.

Lev Yes? But it may be asked whether one can feel proud of living up to one's standards if one perceives that all of one's friends are much better at living up to their standards. Matching one's standards is a matter of degree and also a matter of how high one's standards are. Suppose that when Reuven is thirty he and a group of friends express their disappointment in themselves that they are not devoting enough time to charity work. Each of them resolves to do better, but they do not share their resolutions with each other. Reuven resolves to devote an average of ten hours a month to charity work. Twenty years later Reuven is once again with those friends discussing their charity work. He realizes that over the years he has been about 85 percent successful in keeping his resolution. Suppose his friends divulge their resolutions and their degrees of success in keeping their resolutions. If he finds that most of them resolved to

devote more hours than he and were more successful in keeping
their resolve, he will not feel pride, but if he finds that they resolved
to devote less time or were less successful then he in keeping
the resolve, he may indeed feel pride. I am thinking that in the
background there must always be comparisons to other people.
Even with regard to such a thing as living up to one's standards.

Daniel   Okay, I find that answer pretty convincing. Maybe there
is even a deeper point here about what is meant by "one's own
standards" and how that concept relates to other people. I assume
you'll grant a bit of leeway in this: one's self-esteem need not
constantly feed on consciously comparing oneself to some specific
other people, and one may even temporarily treat as real what one
knows to be only imaginary. But you're claiming that, for there to be
pride or shame, there must be in the background a comparison class
of other people.

Lev   That is my claim. And I hope it needs not saying that
temperamental differences between people would of course influence
which comparisons they focus on and react to. For example, whether
they have a positive or negative outlook. This may affect their self-
esteem greatly. The point can remain that in the background of the
self-assessments that create pride or shame there must be beliefs
about the accomplishments of others. It would therefore be senseless
to talk of the solitary being's feelings of pride or shame.

Daniel   I assume you will make comparable remarks about other
occasions of pride that might on its face seem not to involve other
people. Does a child feel proud of her reading if over a period of time

it improves a lot? You will say, not if the peers to whom she compares herself improve much faster. Perhaps she will be encouraged by parents and teachers to feel proud of her perseverance and toughness in overcoming adversity—but, you will say, not if the peers to whom she compares herself are even more perseverant and tougher. Perhaps she will be encouraged to feel proud of her non-competitiveness, equanimity, go-it-alone spirit, ability to meet her own standards, and so on, but not if . . .

Lev Yes, yes, Daniel. And consider further that even if she sees herself as inferior in every relevant way to the peers she cares about, she may still feel *pleased* or *relieved* that she can read better. But she will not feel *proud*; her self-esteem will not be enhanced. The comparison to other beings outside oneself seems at bottom inevitable if there is to be any such thing as self-esteem. The solitary being too can feel pleased. Solitary beings may feel pleased or displeased, but not proud or ashamed. They are in this respect like dogs.

Daniel It occurred to me to ask whether encouragement or praise itself might somehow generate pride in the absence of any favorable comparisons. Of course, even if this were right, it would not show how a solitary being, who cannot believe that it has received encouragement or praise, might feel proud. After a moment's reflection, moreover, it seems that comparisons are always implicit even in praise: "You are doing well—that is, as compared to other people—other people whom we care about and whom we implicitly treat as the relevant comparison class, people of your age, your training—perhaps, your disability, and so on." A six-year-old child hearing her one-year-old sister being praised for good walking would only be baffled if praise were then lavished on her for much better walking. Comparison to a relevant background comparison class seems always implicit in praise.

Yitzhak   I admit to being impressed. I didn't initially see the point at all, but there certainly is something to the claim Lev is making. But I'm still not convinced. Suppose that my mathematical understanding improves. I have to concede the point that I will not feel proud of my improvement if it is notably inferior to the improvement of the people I normally care about and compare myself to. I might indeed feel quite ashamed of my relatively inferior improvement. But here is an idea: maybe comparison to other people functions as an "enabler" or "disabler."[21] When such comparisons are available they determine whether my self-esteem goes up or down. But when they are not available my self-esteem may be determined by how much I improve or on the degree to which I fulfill difficult resolves. In other words, at any given time a solitary being's self-esteem might be determined by how it views its acts at that time as relating to its acts at previous times. The solitary being may feel proud if it views itself as currently being able to prove theorems faster than it once could.

Daniel   I think you're ignoring the difficulty, Yitzhak. Lev's point is that, if you were a solitary being, what could make you feel proud? Being able to walk, because in the past as a small child you could not do this? Being able to run? Being able to run a mile in four minutes? Being able to count to a hundred because in the past as a small child you could not do this? Being able to add? Being able to prove Fermat's theorem?

Lev Yes, these questions are senseless, I think, and their senselessness reveals that the concept of feeling proud or ashamed can have no meaningful application to a solitary being.

Yitzhak That's too quick. Why don't the same problems arise for us, who are not solitary beings? Why aren't I proud of being able to walk, which makes me superior to small children who can't do it?

Daniel Because it is part of what it means to have a degree of self-esteem that one believes oneself to be connected to a select group of other beings with whom one compares oneself. This is the select group that determines one's sense of self and one's self-esteem. This is Lev's idea and I'm finding it more and more convincing. I am not saying it is easy to explain on what basis this select group is formed, and certainly its contours will not be precise. But it is clear that for a normal adult the group will not consist of small children.

Lev Thank you, Daniel. But allow me now to add a further point. Your self-esteem is connected to your belief in the existence of other people in two ways. There are the people you have to successfully compete against. But there are also the people you wish to impress, the people who judge you, your parents, your teachers, your friends. Of course these two groups may overlap. Your competitors, those you are comparing yourself to, may also be your judges, those you are wishing to impress. But in some manner, of course not easy to explain clearly, your judges greatly influence which the group is that you are to compare yourself to. When you are six years old your parents convey to you that you will not be judged by how your reading compares to your younger sister.

Daniel All of this seems right to me. These background judgmental demands on you from people at the center of your believed world are essential determinants of your degree of self-esteem. Everything in the background of the concept of self-esteem is absent in the solitary being. This is why what you say makes little sense, Yitzhak. The solitary being could have no basis to form a degree of self-esteem by comparing itself to one stage of its past rather than another.

Yitzhak Maybe.

Daniel But let me ask a question here. Might this look different if we adopted Derek Parfit's position? Parfit recommended a way of thinking in which, in place of myself as a being that persists from my birth to my death, and perhaps beyond, I am to be thought of as a self that exists for some short period, and that looks backwards to my "past selves" and forwards to my "future selves."[22] Might that allow the solitary being to compare itself to past and future selves, as we normally compare ourselves to other beings? But as I ask this question I realize that I don't know what I'm talking about. Does the notion of a "solitary being" even make sense in Parfit's way of thinking?

Yitzhak I've never gotten this business about a "different way of thinking." Parfit is simply changing the *language*: instead of saying the words "I once lived in Brooklyn," he recommends the words "Some of my past selves lived in Brooklyn." All of the relevant facts about continuities and connectedness remain the same, and the thesis remains unchanged that there is nothing in personal identity beyond those facts. So how can a change of language amount to anything of significance? In Korsgaard's critique of Parfit's position she says she agrees with his views on the metaphysics of personal identity but she argues that his proposed "way of thinking" will undermine our agency.[23] How could a change of language undermine our agency? Any intention, plan, or policy I express in ordinary terms could simply be translated into Parfit's language. How could that change of language undermine my agency?

Lev   I am not sure if you are right, Yitzhak. A change of language may carry with it a change of phenomenology, a change in the movement of thought, a change in the modes of "seeing as," in the organization of experience, in the *gestalts*, and this may in some cases be significant. But if Parfit's change of language is phenomenologically significant its effect must be as Professor Korsgaard says, to undermine selfhood and agency.

Daniel   But isn't that in a way just what Parfit wants? He takes himself to be defending something like a Buddhist no-self idea.

Lev   *Lo ba-shamayim hi.** I think that Derek Parfit is a brilliant philosopher who seems however lacking phenomenological sensibility.

Yitzhak   "Lacking phenomenological sensibility"! *Azoy!*

Lev   As Spinoza grotesquely arrived at the conclusion that "a free man thinks of nothing less than death,"[24] Parfit, with a rationalist's

---

* *Lo ba-shamayim hi* means "It [the Torah] is not in heaven." Deuteronomy 30:12; *Bava Metzia*, 59b.

argumentative zeal, persuaded himself that it might be an acceptable or even pleasant prospect to undergo fission, to split into two people. There is no serious engagement with the phenomenology of facing the end of one's existence. Lofty arguments devoid of phenomenological insight.

Yitzhak   *Azoy!*

Daniel   I assume that Lev will allow that there are states of ecstasy—mystical or sexual or drug induced—in which the self is in some sense temporarily annihilated. But it's clear that Parfit was not recommending a life of perpetual self-annihilating ecstasy, if indeed there could be such a "life." Nor, I'm sure, is this recommended by Buddhism proper . . . Okay. Good. Maybe we'll have something more to say about Parfit later, but let's for now assume that we are dealing with people like Vatol and us who think of their persistence through time in the normal way, not in the way proposed by Parit. I think we should now go on to your second premise, Lev. This says that a being that has no degree of self-esteem cannot have a self.

The meaning of "having a self"

Yitzhak   One comment I would make is that in this premise, unlike the others you've appealed to, Lev, you seem to be appealing to a somewhat technical notion. Unlike the idea of self-esteem, which is a garden-variety idea understood in some manner by all fluent speakers of the language, the idea of "having a self" seems to me to be an essentially technical notion coming out of psychology.

I remember some time ago looking at this psychology book of readings, and there were papers in there by psychologists about the self as being a "reflection" of how others see you, which sounds a bit like what Lev is saying.[25]

Daniel I don't know if it's a technical notion. Don't you think ordinary people would understand what might be meant by saying "A dog has no self"? I don't know. People also might say "A dog has no identity." Of course that can't mean numerical identity. Along the same lines, if a human being counts as a "person" from birth to death, then it might be said that a person will go through stages of not having a self, or not *being* a self—I assume that's the same thing. During infancy or during extreme dementia one is not a self.

Yitzhak Maybe this doesn't qualify as technical talk, maybe you're right about that, but I certainly think it's very obscure.

Lev I agree that "having a self" is both more technical and more obscure than the idea of having self-esteem. Nevertheless, it has profound relevance to our discussion. We should not seek a reduction, but we may perhaps tie the more obscure concept of self to less obscure concepts. We might tie what it means to have a self to many *self-hyphenated properties*, as one might call them. I mean such properties as self-esteem, self-respect, self-confidence, self-awareness, self-discipline, self-absorption, self-centeredness, self-reliance, and many, many others. These hyphenated properties are not very obscure or technical. And we can say that the self is a configuration of such properties. A little kitten might be shy and fearful, and it may even seem to us that it deliberately renders itself inconspicuous. But we would not say that it is self-effacing. It has no self and it cannot be self-effacing.

Yitzhak   Most kittens are deficient in the area of self-deprecating humor.

Lev   Yes. Self-deprecation. Another example is, a lion hunts its prey with great confidence? Might we say that? Perhaps. But does the lion have much self-confidence? That is very odd to say. The lion has no self and it cannot be self-confident.

Daniel   You're suggesting that we consider these self-hyphenated properties, which we do seem to have some ordinary understanding of, and then broach the concept of the self in terms of such properties. I agree it is a striking fact that many of these self-hyphenated concepts do seem much clearer and more pedestrian than the concept of having or being a self. And speakers of the language learn to understand such terms as "self-confidence," "self-respect," and the like, before they learn to understand the term "having a self," if indeed they ever do learn to understand the latter term. But are you suggesting, Lev, that the *property* of having a self is grounded in these diverse self-hyphenated properties, that the latter properties are *metaphysically prior* to the former?

Lev   As I have said, I do not seek a reduction. I do not speak of metaphysical priorities and grounding. I have little understanding of such doctrines.

Daniel   I see. But I take it you are suggesting that the concept of the self might be understood in terms of a configuration of these rather familiar self-hyphenated properties.

Lev Yes, that is my suggestion.

Daniel But what can be meant here by a "configuration"? Are these properties connected in some distinctive way?

Lev Yes, they are connected as follows: it is impossible to have one of them without having many of the others. For any particular self some will be more central to the configuration than others. But, for any self, there must always be properties of three general categories: awareness of the self, evaluation of the self, and governance of the self. It is impossible to have a degree of any self-hyphenated property without having a degree of these three kinds of properties. The second category includes self-esteem, self-respect, self-confidence and others. I take self-esteem to be the most primitive of these. Respect might be an attitude beyond the capacity of some low-level self, but there can be no self without some degree of self-esteem.

Yitzhak Wait a minute! Why is that impossible? Surely it is conceivable that a being might have a degree of self-awareness without having any degree of self-esteem.

Lev No, that is not conceivable! Let me ask you, Yitzhak. might an object have shape without volume or volume without shape? I think most people would say not. In that same way a being could not have some degree of self-awareness without having some degree of self-esteem.

Yitzhak Well, I don't know what to say about that example. It seems completely different from the thing you're saying.

Lev Might a being have desires without beliefs, or beliefs without desires?

Yitzhak   Okay, I think your point is that there seem to be examples in which distinct properties must necessarily go together. Maybe that is right. But the claim you're making about the necessary connections between these different self-hyphenated properties seems much more puzzling.

Lev   It will seem puzzling to someone whose mind is closed to phenomenological insight.

Daniel   I think you two may be talking past each other. What do we mean by self-awareness? I think what Yitz means by self-awareness is simply the first-person, autobiographical awareness that a person has of that person's career. In Yitz's use a person has self-awareness as long as the person has a lot of true autobiographical beliefs—perhaps we need to add that the beliefs qualify as knowledge. But what Lev means by self-awareness is that the person has a "self-image," and that concept does include evaluative components. To have self-awareness in Lev's sense requires having a degree of self-esteem. Your self-awareness in this sense requires an awareness of "who you are," what your place is in the world, and that certainly involves evaluative attitudes and probably a number of the self-hyphenated properties.

Yitzhak   I see. Then I've got no problem with this. If you're simply packing into what you're calling self-awareness that there's got to be some evaluative self-hyphenated properties, then it will follow trivially that there can't be self-awareness without there being something like self-esteem.

Lev   I am not very happy, Daniel. First, you make too simple what you call an "autobiographical belief." This is not a simple idea. And the familiar stories told by Perry and Kaplan about such beliefs seem to be missing an essential phenomenological component, related to the very issue we are discussing.[26]

Daniel   Actually, there have been published objections to the Perry–Kaplan account that may be related a bit to what is bothering you. These appeared years ago in work by Palle Yourgrau, and more recently in Kripke.[27]

Lev   Yes? Good. What must be abjured, Daniel, is an account that is too reductive. At the outset of part two of the *Investigations* Wittgenstein talks of "patterns which recur in different variations in the weave of our life." The most basic indispensible weave of our life is our *self*. The recurrent patterns are the behaviors exhibiting the self-hyphenated properties. The weave is a *gestalt*, the self-*gestalt*, whose component patterns cannot be separated from the weave.

Yitzhak   *Oy vey.*

Daniel   Okay. Good, good. We haven't said anything directly yet about the third premise, that a being that has no self cannot be intellectually responsible. But I think it's pretty clear what the force of that is, given how Lev is thinking of these matters. A being that has no self has no self-esteem, no self-discipline, no self-criticism. Such a being cannot be a responsible agent in any respect, and, in particular, cannot be a responsible cognitive agent who is committed to standards of truth and reason.

Yitzhak   You know, Lev, I don't quite understand why you even need to get involved with this obscure stuff about having a self.

Unless this is just *yagdil Torah ve-yadir.** Why can't you go directly
from your premise about self-esteem being impossible for the
solitary being, to the conclusion that the solitary being can't be
intellectually responsible? You just need the added premise that a
being who has no degree of self-esteem can't be intellectually
responsible. I suppose that seems plausible enough. An intellectually
responsible being must be committed to standards of truth and
reason. Suppose on some occasion he compromises these standards
to an abysmal degree. Mustn't his self-esteem be undermined? To say
that his self-esteem is not undermined, because the concept of
self-esteem cannot apply to him, seems tantamount to saying that he
is not really committed to those standards. There can't possibly be
anything that deserves to be called *commitment* if one's self-esteem is
not at stake. I don't know. Maybe that's plausible. In any case, I don't
think you're going to squeeze anything better out of this obscure
stuff about "having a self." In fact, it's one thing to claim that self-
esteem requires a background in one's consciousness of others who
compete and judge. That seems more plausible than the claim you're
making, that having a self requires this background of others.

Lev   Be that as it may, that claim is the most crucial point of my
argument. It is indeed even the underlying point of the earlier
argument about valuing one's life. We have the same problem, Yitzhak,
we had earlier. You will not allow yourself to appreciate the void, the
cognitive oblivion, of the solitary being's perspective. The void consists

* In the Talmud it is allowed that infrequently a certain word in the Torah may actually be
superfluous and occurs in order to *yagdil Torah ve-yadir*, i.e., to magnify the Torah and
make it glorious (as in Isaiah 42:21). (See Chullin 66B.)

in just this, the absence of self. Every cognitive breath we take—*Ich mein*, when we are intellectually responsible agents—every cognitive breath we take depends at every moment on the background in our consciousness of other beings, because otherwise the self that is the arena of responsible cognition is necessarily obliterated.

Daniel   That is the hard thing to get, Lev. When I follow the skeptical thoughts of Descartes, Hume, Russell, and the other major people who have written on skepticism about external reality, the posture I'm supposed to adopt, or perhaps pretend to adopt, is, "Here I am, trying as best I can to decide on the basis of reason whether there is anything outside my mind." But what you're trying to say is that this posture is incoherent. If I'm attempting to reason, to reason responsibly—and of course that's what I'm trying to do in philosophy—then there must be a *self* who is trying to reason. And you're saying that there being such a self necessarily depends on my having the very beliefs that my reasoning is trying to call into question. That's the hard thing to get. According to you, it's inconceivable that I should be sitting here asking myself in a responsible manner, "Are there any other people—or lives?"

Yitzhak   I don't understand this business about loss of self. But let me say something else about the simpler argument you could have given from the premises that, first, a solitary being cannot have any degree of self-esteem and that, second, an intellectually responsible agent must have some degree of self-esteem. What I want to mention is that this argument is not vulnerable to one kind of objection I raised to the first argument. I asked why the solitary being could not value its life on probabilistic grounds. That objection can't apply to the present argument. If we accept Lev's idea that one's self-esteem depends on comparing oneself to other people, it can't be objected that these comparisons might be probabilistic. That makes no sense. Suppose that while woozy with a fever you check your email messages before going to bed and see that a distinguished journal has notified you about a paper you submitted. When you wake up the next morning your memory is somewhat hazy. You don't believe outright that the paper was accepted, but you do believe this to a high degree. If this is so you cannot possibly feel proud of having the paper accepted. You cannot say, "It may be that the paper wasn't accepted, but I feel proud that the paper was probably accepted." You may feel hopeful and excited about the likelihood of your success, but you cannot feel proud of having the paper accepted without believing outright that the paper was accepted. By the same token, you can't feel proud of how your behavior compares to other people unless you believe outright that there are other people. Merely believing that probably there are other people could not sustain your self-esteem.

Daniel   So are you persuaded by that argument?

Yitzhak   I'm not convinced that being proud requires a comparison to other people. I don't know what's involved in being proud.

Interlude: Yitzhak's pride and shame

Daniel   Yitzhak is racking his brains to remember the last time he allowed himself to feel proud of something.

Yitzhak   Yeah. Right.

Lev Yitzhak has much to be proud of. Very much.

Yitzhak Do you guys think I can make an arrangement with my lawyer that after I die someone will come by once a month to spit on my grave?

Lev We will need to find for you a Jewish baseball player, Yitzhak, someone who has trained his entire professional life in the delights of spitting. Someone who has trouble restraining himself from spitting when he is visiting his relatives' graves. Such a Jew will perhaps not even demand a fee to provide you with the spitting you require. *Zeh neheneh ve-zeh lo chaser.**

Yitzhak You know, this reminds me of this joke my father used to tell about these two *yidden* who are arguing with each other. One of them says, "*Ich bin a gurnisht*, I'm a nobody." The other guy objects, "*Nein, nein.* No, no. *Du bist a chusheve mensch*, you're a distinguished man, you've published so much, you're cited all over, you've done so many good things. It's me, me, *Ich bin a gurnisht*, I'm a nobody." The first guy insists, "*Nein, adderabbah*, no, on the contrary, *du bist a zeir chusheve mensch*, you're a very distinguished man, you have so many students, you've won so many awards. *Ich, Ich bin a gurnisht.*" And they go back and forth like that. Eventually a third guy interjects, "*Nein, nein,* both of you are very distinguished and accomplished. It's me, me, *Ich bin a gurnisht.*" And they both turn on him furiously: "*Oychet a gurnisht!* Another nobody!"

---

* "One person benefits and the other does not lose." There is a Talmudic controversy in regard to the conditions under which a benefiter who did not lose can exact a fee from the one who benefited. (See *Bava Kamma* 20b.)

Lev   Yes. This is why the solitary being could not feel proud of being a nobody. That especially is an achievement depending on comparing one's disgraces to those of the many other competing nobodies. Richard Moran gives an example of a man who is first ashamed of a bad deed, and then feels proud of being ashamed.[28] But I think only if his friends are not more ashamed of their bad deeds.

Yitzhak   That would be a good title for a memoir: "Oychet A Gurnisht".

Lev   But you will never write a memoir, Yitzhak.

Yitzhak   Why not?

Lev   Will you?

Yitzhak   No.

Relationship between the notions of "self" and "identification"

Daniel   But let me ask you a different question, Lev. When I think of recent philosophical discussions of the self what seems most central to me is the idea of "identification" as this has been discussed by a number of people following Harry Frankfurt.

Yitzhak   *Heshie*?

Daniel   In these discussions the notion of "identification" does not derive in any straightforward way from the concept of the numerical identity of a person, the concept that analytic philosophers since the time of Locke call "personal identity." It relates rather to the sort of identity that defines one's "sense of identity," that defines "who one is," the sort of identity that sustains the central motives that shape one's life and that one can within limits change or lose. One *identifies* with one's desires if, or to the degree that, they are part of "who one is." As Frankfurt has emphasized, in a conflict of desires there may be a sense in which *I-italicized* am on the side of one desire, identifying with it and struggling against the other desire. The desire that I identify with is in some sense what I *really* desire.[29]

Frankfurt initially suggested that identification is simply reflective desire. I am identified with a first-order desire if I have a second-order desire to have that first-order desire. But he soon confronted the question as to what was special about the second-order desire that makes it belong to *me-italicized* in a way that the first-order desire might not belong to *me-italicized*. He offered several answers to this. But I think the best development of Frankfurt's position is found in work by Michael Bratman. Bratman distinguishes between what he calls "weak" and "strong" reflectiveness.[30] I have weak reflectiveness if I have higher order attitudes towards my first-order desires, that is, I am not a "wanton." I have strong reflectiveness if I can "take a stand" with respect to my first-order desires, so that only some first-order desires are *mine-italicized*. Identification, then, is a matter of strong reflectiveness.

The question then is what is required for strong reflectiveness. Bratman proposes the following answer: one has strong reflectiveness if one has "self-governing policies," such policies as, for example, to never act on a desire for revenge. We might say, I think, at least as a first approximation, that a self-governing policy is a general desire to have or not have certain kinds of desires, or a general desire to act or not to act on certain kinds of desires. So it is essentially Frankfurt's reflectiveness at a more general level. One identifies with a desire if it conforms to a self-governing policy; one is alienated from a desire if it flouts a self-governing policy.

Now a question I have is how "identification" relates to "having a self." Might a being satisfy one of these concepts but not the other? If we accept Bratman's account of identification, then I suppose self-governance counts as one of the self-hyphenated properties that might enter into what it means to have a self, so that a condition for identifying is that one have a self. On Frankfurt's initial account, however, it's not immediately clear that a being who can selectively identify with some of its desires must have a self in the sense we were trying to get at. And the other direction is not clear even on Bratman's account: Could a being who has no capacity to identify with some of its desires have a self? That does sound very odd to me, but I'm not sure what to make of it.

Let me say that one reason why I'm eager to bring the notion of identification into this discussion is that I'm eager to get back to an issue we tabled earlier. We said that according to some philosophers, including Peter Strawson and Thomas Nagel, we might doubt external reality at one level while believing at another level. An especially interesting version of that view, I think, is in Janet Broughton.[31] She suggests that Hume did not identify with his belief in external reality; in that sense he did not *really* believe. Lev, I take it, has a problem with this proposal. So I think we need to talk about identification to try to resolve finally what Vatol's epistemic attitude might be, and perhaps what our own attitudes ought to be.

Yitzhak   I think a problem we're having is that we're not tracking any relatively stable concepts. If I'm an unwilling addict, in Frankfurt's famous example, then I'm supposed to say that *I-italicized* didn't want to take the drug, that I *really* didn't want to take it, that I lost my struggle with my desire to take it. But the thing I might actually say is that I *really, really* wanted it so much that I overcame my rational decision not to take it. What does that mean, that the "I" that overcame the decision wasn't the italicized "I"? A lot of this seems to me to be whistling in the dark. There just aren't any stable intuitions in these cases about what *you-italicized* "really" wanted. Suppose you say to the unwilling addict, "Your desire overcame your rational decision, but where did *you* stand in this conflict?" He won't be able to make any sense out of the question; he won't know what you're talking about. That won't help his rehab. So I doubt that there is much of any pre-theoretical notion of "identification" to work with. Of course you can *define* it in terms of Bratman's self-governing policies, but then that's basically nothing but a stipulation.

Daniel   I see your point, Yitzhak, but I think you're overstating it. You may be right—and this is significant—that someone's "really" wanting something may be in one sense simply a matter of the strength of the desire and not whether the desire is being identified with. But it seems that there is another sense of "really" wanting something that does reflect the idea of identification. Someone might say, "My desire to take the drug was overwhelmingly strong, and in its strength overcame my will, but I really didn't want to take it." There we have another sense of "really wanting," and that's the sense relevant to identification. And I don't think that the idea of "where *you* stood in the conflict" is so far removed from ordinary conceptions as to be unrecognizable. If given a multiple-choice question, "Where did *you* stand, for or against taking the drug," I'd bet that the unwilling addict will have little trouble giving the right answer.

Yitzhak   Yeah, maybe you're right. What are you thinking about, Lev?

Lev   I am wondering about Daniel's question as to the relationship between "having a self" and "identification." I am of the opinion that it is likely a mistake to try to separate these different concepts. Indeed I consider it doubtful that a being could possibly have Bratman's weak self-reflexiveness without having strong self-reflexiveness. It is inadequate to rest with the observation that it is not formally derivable from the definitions of these concepts that the first entails the second. The entailment may be "synthetic" rather than "analytic." I would want to say that the entailment is phenomenological. This, I think, is the most central methodological departure of the *Investigations* from the *Tractatus*, that in matters of phenomenology patterns hang together in a manner that cannot readily be captured in terms of formal considerations.

Yitzhak   Wittgenstein the phenomenologist!

Lev   Let us ponder what it means to desire a desire. Why would one desire to have a desire? I am talking about desiring a desire as an end.

Daniel   Frankfurt's "love."

Lev   Yes. Why would one desire to have a desire? Could this be an impulse or an urge? "I suddenly had an urge to pinch his nose." Yes.

"I suddenly had an urge to have a desire to pinch his nose." No, that makes no sense at all, in any readily imaginable context. Nor would it make sense to say, "I had an urge to have the desire to eat some herring." It is likely that everything is already packed into Frankfurt's "reasons of love." It is, I think, likely that such reasons can apply only to a being who has a self-image, and who has plans and policies, including self-governing policies. A being can desire a desire as an end only by seeing the latter desire as conforming to his sense of self, to his sense of what sort of being he is and what the shape of his life is. Having a self and having the capacity to identify with aspects of one's life are inseparably connected to each other and to one's reasons of love, connected, yes, as inseparable patterns in the weave of a life.

Daniel   Then even weak self-reflection will require a belief in interactions with other lives?

Lev   I am inclined to think this. But I am happy to admit that these matters are not very clear in my mind and call for much further thought.

Broughton's suggestion that Hume did not identity with his belief in an external reality

Daniel   Okay, good. Perhaps we can gain some further illumination on these matters by turning to Broughton's suggestion that Hume did not identify with his belief in external reality and therefore did not really believe this. But we should first distinguish her proposal

from another one in the literature. A somewhat different picture
than Broughton's is that Hume had "two moods," he did not believe
in external reality while he philosophized but believed at other
times.[32] Broughton rejects this. She maintains, on the contrary,
that even when Hume was in the philosophy room he could not
completely divest himself of his ordinary belief in an external reality.
This will obviously follow from Lev's position. Lev's central claim is
that we cannot possibly think and philosophize as skeptics about
external reality. It is precisely when one philosophizes that one
attempts to exhibit to a high degree one's capacity as a genuinely
rational being, an intellectually responsible cognitive agent, and it is
just that capacity that necessarily depends on the belief in one's
meaningful interactions with an external reality. Hence, in Lev's view,
it certainly could not be held that Hume did not believe while he was
engaged in philosophy. Yet, according to Broughton, Hume did not
identify with his belief in external reality when he was engaged in
philosophy.

Yitzhak   He did not identify with his belief. Does that mean that he
did identify with his doubts. Certainly, in his philosophy he carries
on a great deal about doubting.

Daniel   Yes, as I understand it, that's Broughton's idea. As the
unwilling addict desires to take the drug but identifies with the
conflicting desire not to take it, Hume, in the philosophy room,
believes in external reality but identifies with the conflicting doubt in
external reality. I take Broughton to be applying in a distinctive way
what we earlier called the two-level view. This involves saying, as Peter
Strawson does, that one may believe in external reality while doubting

"at the level of philosophy," or, as Nagel says in *The View From Nowhere*, that the "objective self" may doubt external reality while the "subjective self" believes?[33] As I understand it Broughton's position also involves the idea of there being two levels, with the significant added twist that Hume "identified" with the philosophical level.

Yitzhak   Here again, I think that all of this stuff is obscure. What does it mean to say that we believe something at one level but doubt it at another level? And, assuming we can understand what that means, what can Broughton mean by saying that we identify with one level rather than another? One point that I think should be clear is that we are not simply talking about different levels of *evidence*. Suppose that blood tests leave it open whether someone has a certain disease, but a CT-scan shows he has the disease. We might say something to the effect that at a hematological level of evidence it can be doubted that he has the disease, but at the level of scanning there is no doubt. But we don't say that the *physicians* doubt at one level and believe at another. The same point holds when there is a conflict between pragmatic and evidential or epistemic reasons. We might say that at the level of evidential considerations the person has reason to doubt that he will survive his surgery but at the level of purely pragmatic considerations he has reason to believe he will survive. That doesn't mean that the person himself is divided between a level at which he doubts and a level at which he believes; he may simply doubt or simply believe. But that's what these philosophers are saying: that we doubt external reality at one level while believing at another. That our minds are in some sense divided into levels. What can that mean? The only thing that I can think of is self-deception, where you in some sense believe something that you don't believe "deep down." Is that what these philosophers are suggesting: that belief in external reality is self-deception?

Daniel   I don't think that's what they mean. But I think you're again exaggerating, Yitzhak. Having conflicting attitudes at different levels seems to be a quite ordinary idea, even in many kinds of examples not involving self-deception. I might resent someone at one level, but not resent him at another level.

Yitzhak   Give me an ordinary example of believing and doubting at different levels, where self-deception doesn't enter into it.

Lev   I will give an example. At night before retiring I go downstairs to check that the door is properly locked. When I ascend the stairs I feel as if someone is peering through the window on the door and may come up behind me to attack me. I often run up the stairs.[34]

Yitzhak   Why does that not surprise me?

Lev   But of course I am not "really" afraid of being attacked. I do not really believe that someone may be behind me. At one level I do believe it, but I do not identify with that level. And let me say what I think this "identification" means. It is the child in me that fears the bogeyman coming up behind me from the dark. My adult self does not believe in such things. And it is my adult self that dominates. For I live my life as an adult, not as a child. The child in me can induce me to run up the stairs. But I do not scream for help. My dominant adult self will not disturb my wife.

Yitzhak The fact that you run up the stairs but won't scream could be explained in decision theoretic terms: the degree of credence you assign to the proposition that the bogeyman is coming up behind you warrants running up the stairs but not waking your wife.

Daniel Yitzhak, I think the point of the example was not to provide an analysis of what it is for there to be conflicting levels or parts of a person. I think that phenomenon has to be accepted as primitive. It seems clear that the example succeeds, since it seems clear that this is not a case of having an unconflicted probabilistic belief. Lev, *he-italicized*, believes outright that no monster is coming up behind him, but at some level he does not have this belief. That was the sort of example you asked for.

Yitzhak Fine, I'll accept that. So the level that is identified with is the level that is dominant in one's life. Surely the level that was dominant in Hume's life was the level of belief, not the level of doubt. He lived his life as a normal person, with the beliefs of a normal person. So what does Broughton mean by saying that he identified with his doubts? In the case of desire the idea was that one identifies with the desire that is endorsed by a second-level desire or, in Bratman, a certain kind of second-level policy. That idea of identification doesn't seem relevant to Broughton's claim about Hume. Since he believed that philosophy leads to this suicidal doubt, he surely had no desire to allow his reasoning to dominate his life with any such philosophical doubt. Hume was surely not like an unwilling addict, addicted to the beliefs that "nature" instilled. If anything he was a willing addict. So what does Broughton mean by saying that he did not identify with his beliefs in external reality?

Lev   I too am not unwillingly addicted to having childish beliefs in my child-level. I do not wish to kill the child in me. I cannot always wait for *Purim* and *Simchas Torah*.[35]

Daniel   I don't think, in general, that whether you desire to have a belief determines whether you "really" have it. Someone may prefer to believe he can be cured when the evidence forces him to believe that he has a fatal disease. He may prefer to believe falsely that the disease is not fatal. He may *value* having that belief. But he clearly "really" believes that the disease is fatal. So it is clear from every angle that if Hume identified with his doubts, as Broughton holds, this was not because of what he desired to believe.

Yitzhak   It seems that Broughton is simply assuming that Hume had to identify with the doxastic attitude that he took his reason to endorse. What I suspect is that she is implicitly talking about self-deception. She may be assuming that a belief that you take not to be endorsed by reason is a self-deceptive belief, a belief that you don't "really" have, in that "deep down" you doubt.

Daniel   But that point could not justify what Broughton says about Hume's identification with his doubts. When you deceive yourself you identify with the self-deceptive belief, not with the doubt that you're concealing from yourself. Sartre's anti-Semite did not identify with his deep-down favorable beliefs about Jews, but with his self-deceiving anti-Semitic beliefs.[36] The anti-Semitic level dominates in the same sense in which Lev's adult level dominates: that is the level by which the anti-Semite lives. The same would apply to Hume's belief in external reality, even if this belief is viewed as self-deceptive. He identifies with the belief even if deep down he doubts.

Yitzhak So all of this is a total mess. We seem to have three
different kinds of "conflicting levels," and a thoroughly fragmented
notion of "identification." In Frankfurt's examples conflicting
levels of desire involve a second-order desire versus a first-order
desire, the former desire counting as the one identified with, and
counting as what one "really" desires. In Lev's example the two
levels of belief have apparently nothing to do with first-order versus
second-order. There is just, as Danny said, a primitive idea of two
levels. And in this case the level identified with is the one that
dominates in the person's life. The beliefs at that level are the ones
the person "really" has. Notice that the unwilling addict's desire may
dominate in his life, but that apparently doesn't get Frankfurt or his
followers to allow that the unwilling addict identifies with his
addiction or "really" has the addictive desire. Finally, there is the
case of self-deception, in which the deep-down belief conflicts
with the self-deceptive belief. In this case it seems that the
deep-down belief is the one "really" had, but not the one identified
with. A total mess.[37]

Daniel Perhaps merely a mess of ambiguities that can be cleared
up, Yitzhak.

Yitzak But maybe none of this matters very much in understanding
Lev's position, since I think Lev is going to say that there can't
possibly be a philosophical level of doubt. Any philosophical level has
to be a level of responsible reasoning, and that requires a background
of belief in other lives. Is that right, Lev?

Lev Yes.

Lev's epistemic attitude

Daniel   I'm now understanding something that has puzzled me
the whole time. Hume says that what prevents us from doubting
is our nature. That must mean certain contingent facts of human
psychology. This is apparently the view of Nagel and probably various
other philosophers. When these philosophers say it's impossible to
doubt, they are appealing to some contingent principles of human
psychology. I've been puzzled by why Lev insists on presenting his
case for the impossibility of doubt as a metaphysical impossibility.
Why couldn't he have made the points about Vatol's inarticulate
anxiety more simply by appealing, as these other philosophers do, to
contingent psychology? But the answer I now see is that empirical
psychology may rule out doubt at the level of life while leaving it
open that doubt is possible at the philosophical level. That is what
Lev's arguments rule out as metaphysically impossible.

Yitzhak   I think there is a more basic virtue in Lev's trying to
argue for the a priori metaphysical impossibility of doubting
external reality. The appeal to contingent psychology seems bogus.
What empirical evidence is there for the claim that doubt is not
possible even at the level of living one's life? Maybe one could live
as a solipsist, calculating the course of one's experiences in the
way Berkeley said, or live as someone who has only a probabilistic
belief in external reality. There is no empirical evidence that this is
impossible. We would need to raise a number of children with Vatol's
experiences and see what happens. Where are the Nazis when you
need them? But Lev bypasses these problems with his claim that

such doubts at the level of responsible thought are metaphysically impossible.

So where are we? Where are we with Vatol's anxiety? He can't doubt at any level, according to Lev. So what is he anxious about?

Lev That question has a familiar ring.

Daniel You just said that, according to Lev, Vatol can't doubt at any level. That's not really what we've arrived at. What we've arrived at is that, according to Lev, Vatol can't doubt at the level of philosophical thought or at any level of responsible reasoning. His responsible reasoning pushes him towards the conclusion that he may be a vat-person. Yet he cannot possibly accept this conclusion at the level of responsible reasoning. Would it make any sense to suggest that he *can* accept it at a level at which he does not reason responsibly?

Lev We must distinguish between two questions. The first is whether a being who is not intellectually responsible—Can we perhaps call this a sub-rational being?—our first question is whether a sub-rational being can arrive at a doubt about external reality. The second question is whether an intellectually responsible being such as Vatol might doubt at a sub-rational level, I mean a level at which he is not intellectually responsible. Now it must be borne in mind that to doubt the truth of a proposition is not the same as merely not believing that the proposition is true. A dog does not doubt God's existence, though it does not believe in God's existence. To doubt a proposition is to understand it, in some sense to entertain it, while at the same time not believing it. It is, I would think, possible for there to be a sub-rational being who does not believe in external reality.

Piaget claimed that young children are in this condition. Piaget did not of course say that young children doubt external reality. Piaget's infants are one kind of solitary being, the kind that neither believes in external reality nor doubts it. I assume that a sub-rational being could be this kind of solitary being. As for whether a sub-rational being might be a solitary being who *doubts* external reality, I have trouble imagining this. Consider, first, doubting sense-experience for a period of time. Certainly we can do this, if we are forewarned that, for example, our brains will be temporarily connected to a computer. Might a dog temporarily doubt its sense experience? It is difficult to imagine this. A dog is a sub-rational being that has no commitment, no general policy, to pursue the truth. What could then induce it to reject the bidding of its sense experience, to repudiate its spontaneous perceptual beliefs, for a period of time? If this is not possible even for a period of time, then it is certainly not possible for a dog to reject all of its sense experience, past, present, and future, and thereby doubt external reality.

Daniel   This is related to the point I made earlier, that an intellectual wanton who merely responds to evidence without having any general commitment to truth and reason could probably not be motivated to engage in epistemological reflection.

Yitzhak   Listen. Who's this? "Why don't dogs doubt that the world exists? Because they're too commonsensical?" Not Schlegel.

Lev   Let me say that much remains unclear in my mind about the beliefs and doubts of sub-rational beings. But Vatol is not a sub-rational being; we have assumed that he remains an intellectually responsible being. As an intellectually responsible being he cannot doubt external reality. That has been my argument. Our question now is whether an intellectually responsible being such as Vatol might doubt at a sub-rational level, I mean a level at which he is not intellectually responsible. And I am inclined to answer that there cannot be a level in Vatol of what can properly be called doubt of external reality. But there may be within him a sub-rational level of something related to doubt. Perhaps the shadow of doubt. Vatol's responsible reasoning pushes him towards a doubt that would necessarily destroy responsible reasoning. Vatol's responsible reasoning propels him therefore beyond the level of responsible reasoning to another level at which he feels something that he cannot conceptualize. The shadow of doubt, let us call it. And it is this that engulfs Vatol in an anxiety that has no intelligible object.

Yitzhak   Doubt. The shadow of doubt. Call it "schmdoubt." It's the same thing. What you're really saying is what I said from the start: Down deep Vatol doubts. He gets through life by deceiving himself, by concealing from himself this doubt that would make him insane.

Daniel   I think you're missing the point, Yitzhak. Vatol's reasoning pushes him towards the conclusion that it may all be a hallucination. That's given. We're trying to work out the implication of Lev's claim that this is a conclusion that cannot possibly take hold as a belief in Vatol's consciousness insofar as he is an intellectually responsible being. The suggestion is that the conclusion is therefore shunted off to a sub-rational level at which Vatol is intellectually wanton. At that level he lacks a belief in other lives, and therefore values nothing, has no self-esteem or any other self-hyphenated attitude, he is not

committed to the pursuit of truth or reason, he exercises no control
over his mind. Can we understand what it could mean for him to
"doubt external reality" at that level? Maybe this is partly just a
matter of terminology, but I think Lev is saying that an attitude—a
doxastic attitude, if you will—that cannot possibly take hold within
Vatol's consciousness as an intellectually responsible being is not an
attitude of "doubt" in the ordinary sense of the word.

Yitzhak   So what *is* going on at that "sub-rational" level? The
"shadow of doubt"? What does that mean?

Lev   What is going on at that level? That this question cannot be
answered in any fully intelligible manner is close to the central point.
Vatol too cannot answer it. For you are right, Yitzhak, that we are
dealing here with something akin to self-deceit. Vatol cannot face up
to the void at the sub-rational level. However, this is not a standard
case of self-deceit. In the standard case it is possible, even if difficult,
to face up to the truth. But it is impossible for Vatol to face up to that
sub-rational level within himself that attempts to respond to Reason's
demand for doubt. To face a truth, or to refuse to face it in self-deceit,
is something that can only pertain to an intellectually responsible
being. Yes, that is most plausible, I think. A dog can neither deceive
itself nor face the truth. To face a truth is to incorporate it into
self-consciousness, to incorporate it into a level of cognitive agency,
of intellectual responsibility. Therefore, for Vatol to face up to the
shadow of doubt within him would be to integrate it into his life as an
intellectually responsible being. But that is impossible. In this instance
what is in the shadow must remain in the shadow, for to bring it to
the light of self-consciousness would require it to be a genuine doubt,

which is not a possibility at the level of self-consciousness and intellectual responsibility. This is why neither Vatol nor we can describe the phenomenological void that permeates his existence with anxiety as he goes forth in his life.

Yitzhak   As he goes forth in his life! Go forth, my son. *A bissel* abyss isn't so bad, but avoid a void. Now, *lech lecha*!* Look, this is getting pretty complicated, isn't it? You're agreeing now that Vatol is deceiving himself, but you're saying that the thing he is deceiving himself about is that sub-rational level within him, a level of something like insanity, at which level there is something like doubt. That's what he can't face, you're saying. But that seems to imply that deep down he is that demented sub-rational being, that *really* he does have that doubt, or schmdoubt, or shadow doubt, and he's concealing this fact from himself. Is that what you want to say?

Lev   No, Yitzhak, that is not what I am saying. This is a kind of example in which the different senses of "really" that you mentioned earlier clash with each other. Consider another example. A man anxiously runs up the stairs at night as I do. He is aware of his anxiety but he conceals from himself the fact that when he is anxious this is because he has at some level a belief that the bogeyman is coming up behind him. That fact threatens his self-image and he refuses to face it. Or perhaps he even deceives himself about his anxiety, telling himself that he is feeling eagerness and excitement to return to his apartment.

---

* "A bissel" means in Yiddish "a little bit (of)." "Lech lecha" means in Hebrew "Go (forth)"; these are among the first words (hence the name) of portion (*parshah*) 3 (chapter 12) of Genesis, said by God to Abraham.

Yitzhak   Maybe he tells himself that before he goes to bed he wants to finish up a piece of *gemara* he had been learning. About *bi'ah she-lo ke-darkah*.*

Lev   Then we might say, "He really believes that the bogeyman is behind him". But of course there is another sense in which he does not "really" believe this, as we said that I do not really believe it when I run up the stairs. His dominant belief is as mine, that there is no bogeyman. The level of belief that he conceals from himself is not the dominant one. What we are saying is, "He really believe at some level that the bogey man is behind him, but he conceals this level of belief from himself." This is compatible with saying in another sense of "really believes" that he does not really believe in the bogeyman. That is how it may be with Vatol. Perhaps the dominant level that governs his life is one in which he believes in his interactions with other lives. He is therefore not "really" the demented, sub-rational being. But he "really" contains within himself a sub-rational level containing a form of doubt that he cannot possibly face, but that fills him with anxiety.

Yitzhak   Why do you say it can't be faced? If I'm Vatol and I've been convinced by the story you just told, I don't conceal anything from myself. I face the fact that there is within me at a sub-rational level this shadow doubt that haunts me. I face it.

Lev   No, Yitzhak, you do not face it. You cannot possibly face it. Consider again the man we were just discussing. Suppose he is

---

* "Bi'ah she-lo ke-darkah" refers to unorthodox sexual practices.

persuaded by a psychiatrist that he has anxiety that is caused by a level of belief in the bogeyman. He still has not faced that belief. When I run up the stairs I am conscious of the level of belief that the bogeyman is behind me. But this person, having been persuaded by the psychiatrist that he has that level of belief, has still not brought it into self-consciousness. He still conceals it from himself. Vatol may come to believe that there is within him at a sub-rational level a form of doubt, but he cannot possibly bring it fully to self-consciousness, for that would mean the obliteration of self-consciousness. That is the sense in which he cannot say what he is anxious about, for the object of his anxiety cannot possibly be faced. Yet a glimpse of the oblivion of that subterranean level is possible for Vatol, and for us.

Daniel The man who runs up the stairs while deceiving himself into thinking that he is not anxious, but eager and excited; perhaps that is in some ways analogous to pretending that what one feels is not skeptical anxiety, but is instead a feeling related to irony.

Lev Yes, perhaps. And this self-deceit might be related to the other pretense, the one that I suffered from in my Berkeley days: the conceit that there is an intellectually distinguished level of oneself that is a doubting philosopher, the vaunted objective self of Thomas Nagel that conforms from on high to the demands of reason.

Yitzhak When actually the demands of reason are fobbed off to a lowly sub-rational schmdoubting level. Is that it? But you know, this business of our existence floating on an abyss, on a void, on oblivion, that's what you're really after, Lev, isn't it? You're just aching to use the word "tragic," aren't you? As in "our tragic situation."

Lev   I am able to restrain myself. With your continuing help, Yitzhak.

Daniel   Well, tragic or not, this is our situation, according to Lev: It's possible, metaphysically possible, for us to be completely deceived about our interactions with other lives. And this gives us reason to doubt the reality of those interactions. But it's impossible for us to doubt the reality of those interactions. And this leaves us with a peculiar kind of inarticulate anxiety and bewilderment.

Yitzhak   "A peculiar kind of inarticulate anxiety and bewilderment." That reminds me of Larkin's "special way of being afraid."[38] About death. But I see you've now switched from talking about Vatol to talking about *us*. And that's where I think something completely crazy comes into this. Vatol's situation *is* tragic. If I am in Vatol's situation I don't know if I could remain sane. Maybe I could. I don't know. I noticed before that Lev didn't assume that Vatol's so-called dominant level was the one at which he believes. I guess that would depend on lots of things about Vatol's psychological makeup.

Lev   Yes, I think that is so.

Yitzhak   Yeah. Right. Vatol may bounce in and out of oblivion. Bouncing in and out of oblivion. Once he's in, what would get him out? I guess his bounciness . . . But to claim that our situation is like Vatol's seems to me sheer madness. But that's what you're saying, Lev. At least when we immerse ourselves deeply and seriously in the Cartesian reflection, we're just like Vatol. Is that what you're really saying, Lev? Because I just can't stand that. It's not just crazy to equate our situation to Vatol's. It's *sinful*.

Daniel   And will it stop being sinful if we read at some future point that there are persons on other planets who have created multiple vat-people?

Yitzhak   I can't get back into that argument! But it's impossible for me to believe that we're like Vatol. That's just sick!

Daniel   I guess we're back where we started from. Lev will say that some things can be expressed only in metaphor and poetry.

Yitzhak   Right. Right. Look, let me ask you something, Lev. We haven't been talking much about the concept of knowledge. Let me ask you something. Would you say that you *know* that you and I are standing here talking to each other right now?

Lev   I use the word "know" as J. L. Austin does in "Other Minds."[39] He talks of knowing well enough, knowing for the purposes at hand. He is, I have been told, one of the great mavens of the English language.

Yitzhak   Look, don't give me that bull! I'm asking you simply: Do you know that we're standing here talking to each other?

Lev   I am reminded of a joke that I sometimes attempt on my students. I say to them, "Please raise your hand and tell us two things that you are now deceiving yourself about."

[Prolonged silence.]

Daniel   I think we're about finished.

Yitzhak   That's true. But death is not our topic.

Lev   When I was younger I used to think that I could make a name for myself on death.

Daniel   A name for yourself on death?

Yitzhak   *Oy vey.*

Daniel   Listen, *kinder*, I think we do have to stop now. People have been waiting to get in here.

Lev   I did not realize.

Yitzhak   Many Jews are waiting, waiting, waiting to go to the bathroom.

Daniel   We'll have to continue this another time.

Yitzhak   *Chas ve-shalom.*

NOTES

Act I

1 Incidental expressions of Hebrew or Yiddish will often in their first occurrences be translated in brackets. The relatively few expressions that recur are appended in a short glossary (this seemed preferable to repeating their translations). Ideally, readers will remember the meanings or occasionally glance at the glossary. It should be understood that these incidental expressions have no substantive effects on the philosophical arguments.

2 Descartes (1641). "I am in turmoil, as if I have accidentally fallen into a whirlpool . . ."

3 Hume (1978 [first published 1739]), at p. 269 and p. 218. Hume's attitude towards doubt is in fact ambiguous. More will be said about this in Act III.

4 Strawson (1985), p. 11.

5 "The Absurd," in Nagel (1979), pp. 18–20; Nagel (1986), pp. 88–9.

6 Wittgenstein (1953), p. 224.

7 James (1958 [first published 1902]), p. 326. Cf. Hirsch (2009).

8 James, *ibid.*, Lectures IV–VII.

9 Williamson (2000), p. 165.

10 Ethics of the Fathers, 3.13.

11 Psalms 11:10.

12 Exodus, 3.6.

13 Sosa (2007).

14 Williamson (2007), p. 249.

15 Williamson (2007), pp. 278–92.

16 Beckett (1983).

17 "Four Forms of Skepticism," in Moore (1959), p. 195.

18 Broughton (2004).

19 Epicurus, "Letter to Menoeceus," in Oates (1940).

20 E.g., Kelly (2002).

21 Marušić (2012); Marušić (2015).

22 Putnam (1981).

23 Kripke (1971), pp. 162–3; Kripke (1980), pp. 151–2. Cf. Hirsch (2010); Nagel (1986), p. 73.

24 On these two kinds of "contexts," see, e.g., Hawthorne (2003).

25 See, e.g., Austin (1946); DeRose (1996); Heller (1989); Lewis (1996).

26 Fantl and McGrath (2009).

27 Nozick (1981), pp. 167–288.

28 See "Nozick on Knowledge" in Kripke (2011).

29 Williams (1982).

30 Williamson (2000), ch. 11.

31 However, complications in the relationship between assertion and certainty are noted in Williamson (2000), p. 254.

32 Austin (1946) speaks of "knowing well enough," "knowing for the purposes at hand"; the stakes matter, as for Fantl and McGrath (2009), but in a somewhat different way. Compare with Schaffer (2005). See also "degrees of outright belief" in Williamson (2000), p. 99.

33 Rashba (Rabbi Shlomo ben Aderet, 1235–1310) in Nedarim 2a.

34 Adler (2002), ch. 7. Compare with Stanley (2008).

35 Some have even claimed that the strong sense of belief is essentially a technical notion: see Hawthorne et. al. (2016).

36 See Kaplan (1996); Christensen (2004).

37 See especially below, pp. 168, 196.

38 Williamson (2000), p. 243.

39 Marušić (2013). See Williamson (2000), pp. 260–1.

40 Stroud (1984), especially pp. 31–2.

41 Beckett (1949a). These exact words are actually not in *Waiting For Godot*, though the sentiment as well as the words "I can't go on" are prominent in it. "You must go on, I can't go on, I'll go on" is the final sentence of Beckett's *The Unnamable* (1953).

42 Wittgenstein (1969).

43 2 Samuel 1:19.

44 Beckett (1949b).

45 Feyerabend (1975).

46 Pascal (1672), p. 513.

47 Burnyat (1983).

48 See Marušić (2010).

Act II

1 See Williamson (2000), pp. 123–8.

2 Goldman (1976) presents the famous example in which barn-facades are mistaken for barns.

3 Pryor (2000); Pryor (2001); Pryor (2004).

4 Searle (1983), ch. 2; Siegel (2010).

5 White R. (2006), at 552–3. Related views are in Alston (1985), and Wright (2004).

6 Pryor (2000), p. 547, n37; Pryor (2004), p. 357.

7 McDowell (1994); Martin (2002).

8 James (1958 [first published 1902]), p. 65.

9 Cf. the distinction between undercutting and rebutting defeaters in Pollock (1986).

10 Hawthorne (2003).

11 Cf. Enoch, et al. (2012).

12 See *Makos*, 5a.

13 *Shevuos* 42a.

14 See the discussions of Rambam (Moses Maimonides, 1135–1204), *Mishneh Torah*, Laws of *Eydus*, chapter 18.2.

15 Alston (1991).

16 Egan and Elga (2005).

17 See Sosa (2007) for a view that dreams do not involve delusive beliefs.

18 Pryor's position in Pryor (2000), (2001), and (2004) is not primarily directed to the dreaming argument but quite clearly is meant to encompass that argument. An explicit reference to the dreaming argument is in Pryor (2000), p. 524.

19 Leite (2011). See also Leite (2010), (2013). There are similarities, but also differences, between Leite's view and Yitzhak's.

20 Williamson (2000), ch. 8.

21 See the papers in Christensen and Lackey (2013).

22 Kelly (2005) maintains that the actual existence of a disagreeing epistemic peer has no more epistemic significance than the possible existence of such a peer. If actual or possible vat-people can be epistemic peers of normal people, then, if Vatol's problem derives from issues of disagreement, Kelly's view might support Lev's claim that there is no epistemic difference between Vatol and us. As stated in the text, however, it may not be very plausible to suppose that Vatol's problem does derive from issues of disagreement.

23 Classic formulations are in Nagel (1970) and Nagel (1986).

24 Nagel (1997).

25 Unamuno (1962 [originally published 1921]), p. 114.

26 Shakespeare, *Othello,* Act 5, Scene 2.

27 Cf. Burge (1993).

Act III

1 From a popular song recorded by Otis Redding in 1967.

2 Samuel Johnson famously kicked a stone and said, "I refute it *thus*" in reference to Berkeley's idealism.

3   Plantinga (1967).

4   *Ethic of The Fathers* 1.6.

5   Wittgenstein (1969), p. 492, p. 494, pp. 613–14.

6   Frankfurt (2004).

7   At the end of the Synopsis of the *Meditations* Descartes (1641) says: "[T]hat there is a world, that men have bodies, and other similar things . . . have never been doubted by any man of sound mind."

8   "The Importance of What We Care About" in Frankfurt (1988).

9   Malcolm (1952), p. 276.

10 See Watson (1987): "Notoriously, judging good has no invariable connection to motivation. . . . One can in an important sense fail to value what one judges valuable" (p. 150). See, also, Harman (2000); Bratman (2000a).

11 See the notion of "conditional desire" in Parfit (1986), p. 151.

12 In Bratman (2000a): "an important kind of valuing involves higher order policies" (p. 260), and "the agent's reflective valuing involves a kind of higher order willing" (p. 261). See "Dispositional Theories of Value" in Lewis (2000), and "Desired Desires" in Harman (2000).

13 Gibbard (1990), p. 132.

14 See Williamson, (2000), p. 21.

15 Compare with Dancy (2000), pp. 131ff.

16 Wittgenstein (1953), section 420.

17 James (1896).

18 Rav Aharon Kotler (1891–1962) was one of the most prominent Talmudists of the twentieth century. The reference is to *Mishnat Rebbi Aharon* (*Zeraim, Taharot*), chapter 31.1.

19 In section 6 of Book 2 of the *Treatise*, Hume says that an agreeable object causes pride only if it is "peculiar to ourselves, or at least common to us with a few persons"; otherwise it "loses its value" because it is "often presented." That may suggest that the absence of other people would make pride easier to come by.

20 Sartre (1966 [originally published 1943]), part 3, chapter 1, section 4 ("The Look").

21 Dancy (2006) discusses "enabling." The suggestion in the text comes from Beri Marušić.

22 Parfit (1986).

23 Korsgaard (1989).

24 Spinoza (1919 [originally published 1677]), E4, Prop 67.

25 See Tice and Wallace (2003).

26 Kaplan (1989); Perry (1993).

27 Yourgrau (1982); "The First Person" in Kripke (2011).

28 Moran (2001), pp. 174–5.

29 The notion of identification has been discussed in a number of places, including Frankfurt (2004); Frankfurt (1988); Bratman (2000a); Bratman (2000b); Bratman (1999); Watson (1982); Jaworska (2007). See also the notion of "volitional identity" in Frankfurt (2004), p. 22, and the notion of "practical identity" in Korsgaard (1996).

30 Bratman (2000b), p. 38.

31 Broughton (2004).

32 Broughton (2004), note 21.

33 Strawson (1985); Nagel (1986), pp. 67–74.

34 Compare with the examples of "alief" in Gendler (2008).

35 Two holidays during which Jewish law permits adults to engage in forms of childish behavior, such as pranks and mimicry.

36 Sartre (1965 [originally pubished1946]).

37 Compare with Knobe (2011).

38 Philip Larkin, *Aubade*.

39 Austin (1946).

GLOSSARY

Apikoros   apostate
Azoy!   Really!
Azoy vee mir zugt   as one says
Chas ve-shalom   heaven forbid
chiluk   distinction
halachah   Jewish law
her zich ein   listen
Ich mein   I mean
kinas sofrim   envy of scholars
kinder   children
le-chumra   stringently
le-kula   leniently
mamash   literally
mefarshim   commentators
sevara   rationale
tefillin   phylacteries

REFERENCES

Adler, J. 2002. *Belief's Own Ethics* (MIT Press, Cambridge, Ma.).

Alston, W. P. 1985. "Thomas Reid on Epistemic Principles," *History of Philosophy Quarterly* 2, 435–51.

—— 1991. *Perceiving God: The Epistemology of Religious Experience* (Cornell University Press, Ithaca, NY).

Austin, J. L. 1946. "Other Minds," *Proceedings of the Aristotelian Society*, Supplementary Volume XX. Reprinted in Austin's *Philosophical Papers*, 3rd edition, (Oxford University Press, NY, 1979), pp. 76–116.

Beckett, S. 1949a. *Waiting For Godot* (Grove Press, NY [1954]).

—— 1949b. "Three Dialogues," *Transition*, no. 5.

—— 1953. *The Unnamable* (Grove Press, NY [1958]).

—— 1983. *Worstward Ho* (Calder Publications, London).

Bratman, M. 1999. *Faces of Intention: Selected Essays on Intention and Agency* (Cambridge University Press, NY).

—— 2000a. "Valuing and the Will," *Philosophical Perspectives* 14, 49–65.

—— 2000b. "Reflection, Planning, Agency," *Philosophical Review* 109, 35–61.

Broughton, J. 2004. "The Inquiry in Hume's Treatise," *Philosophical Review* 113(4), 537–56.

Burge, T. 1993. "Content Preservation," *Philosophical Review* 102 (4):457–88.

Burnyat, M. ed. 1983. *The Skeptical Tradition* (University of California Press, Berkeley, Calif.).

Christensen, D. 2004. *Putting Logic in its Place: Formal Constraints on Rational Belief* (Oxford University Press, NY).

Christensen, D. and Lackey, J. eds. 2013. *The Epistemology of Disagreement* (Oxford University Press, N.Y.)

Corey, W. J. 1905 (first published 1891). "Heraclitus" in *Ionica* (George Allen, London).

Dancy, J. 2000. *Practical Reality* (Oxford University Press, Oxford).

—— 2006. *Ethics Without Principles* (Oxford University Press, Oxford).

DeRose, K. 1996. "Relevant Alternatives and the Content of Knowledge Attributions," *Philosophy and Phenomenological Research* 56: 193–7.

Descartes, R. 1641. *Meditations On First Philosophy* (Hackett Publishing Co., Indianapolis [1979]).

Egan, A. and Elga, A. 2005. "I Can't Believe I'm Stupid," in *Philosophical Perspectives* 19/1, 77–93.

Enoch, D., Spectre, L., and Fisher, T. 2010. "Statistical Evidence, Sensitivity, and the Legal Value of Knowledge," *Philosophy & Public Affairs* 40, 3, 197–224.

Fantl, J. and McGrath, M. 2009. *Knowledge In An Uncertain World* (Oxford University Press, NY).

Feyerabend, P. 1975. *Against Method* (New Left Books, London).

Frankfurt, H. 1988. *The Importance of What We Care About* (Cambridge University Press, NY).

—— 2004. *Reasons of Love* (Princeton University Press, Princeton, NJ).

Gendler, T. S. 2008. "Alief and Belief," *The Journal of Philosophy* 105, 634–63.

Gibbard, A. 1990. *Wise Choices, Apt Feelings* (Harvard University Press, Cambridge, Mass.).

Goldman, A. 1976. "Discrimination and Perceptual Knowledge," *The Journal of Philosophy* 73, 771–91.

Harman, G. 2000. *Explaining Value* (Oxford University Press, Oxford).

Hawthorne, J. 2003. *Knowledge and Lotteries* (Oxford University Press, Oxford).

Hawthorne, J., Rothschild, D., and Spectre, L. 2016. "Belief Is Weak," *Philosophical Studies* 173 (5), 1393–1404.

Heller, M. 1989. "Relevant Alternatives," *Philosophical Studies* 55: 23–40.

Hirsch, E. 2009. "Diabolical Mysticism, Death, and Skepticism," *Philosophic Exchange*, Vol. 39, Iss. 1, Article 3.

—— 2010. "Kripke's Argument Against Materialism" in R. C. Koons and G. Bealer, eds., *The Waning of Materialism* (Oxford University Press, NY).

Hume, D. 1978 (first published 1739). *A Treatise of Human Nature*, ed., L. A. Selby-Bigge, 2nd edition (Oxford University Press, Oxford).

James, W. 1896. "The Will to Believe," *The New World*, Vol. 5, 327–47.

—— 1958. (first published 1902). *The Varieties of Religious Experience*, Mentor Edition (The New American Library of World Literature, NY).

Jaworska, A. 2007. "Caring and Internality," *Philosophy and Phenomenological Research* 74 (3), 529–68.

Kaplan, D. 1989. "Demonstratives" in J. Almog, J. Perry, and H. Wettstein, eds., *Themes from Kaplan* (Oxford University Press, NY).

Kaplan, M. 1996. *Decision Theory As Philosophy* (Cambridge University Press, NY).

Kelly, T. 2002. "The Rationality of Belief and Some Other Propositional Attitudes," *Philosophical Studies* 110: 163–96.

—— 2005. "The Epistemic Significance of Disagreement" in J. Hawthorne and T. Gendler, eds., *Oxford Studies in Epistemology* (Oxford University Press, NY) pp. 167–96.

Knobe, J. 2011. *N.Y. Times, The Stone*, https://opinionator.blogs.nytimes.com/2011/06/05/in-search-of-the-true-self.

Korsgaard, C. 1989. "Personal identity and the Unity of Agency: A Kantian Response to Parfit," *Philosophy and Public Affairs* 18, no. 2, 101–32.

—— 1996. *The Sources of Normativity* (Cambridge University Press, Cambridge).

Kripke, S. 1971. "Identity and Necessity" in M. K. Munitz, ed., *Identity and Individuation* (NYU Press, NY, 1971); reprinted in J. Kim and E. Sosa, eds, *Metaphysics* (Blackwell, Oxford, 1999).

—— 1980. *Naming and Necessity* (Harvard University Press, Cambridge, Ma.).

—— 2011. *Philosophical Troubles* (Oxford University Press, N.Y.).

Leite, A. 2010. "How To Take Skepticism Seriously," *Philosophical Studies* Vol. 148, No. 1, 39–60.

—— 2011. "Austin, Dreams, and Scepticism," in M. Gustafsson and R. Sørli, eds., *The Philosophy of J.L. Austin* (Oxford University Press), pp. 78–113.

—— 2013. "But That's Not Evidence; It's Not Even True," *The Philosophical Quarterly*, Vol. 63, No. 250, 81–104.

Lewis, D. 1996. "Elusive Knowledge," *Australasian Journal of Philosophy* 74: 549–67.

—— 2000. *Papers in Ethics and Social Philosophy* (Cambridge University Press, NY).

Malcolm, N. 1952. "Knowledge and Belief," *Mind* 61 (242): 178–89.

Martin, M. 2002. "The Transparency of Experience," *Mind and Language* 17 (4), 376–425.

Marušić, B. 2010. "Skepticism Between Excessiveness and Idleness," *European Journal of Philosophy* 18.1, 60–83

—— 2012. "Belief and Difficult Action," *Philosopher's Imprint*, Vol. 12, No. 18, 1–30.

—— 2013. "The Self-Knowledge Gambit," *Synthese*, Vol. 190, No. 12, 1977–99.

—— 2015. *Evidence and Agency: Norms of Belief for Promising and Resolving* (Oxford University Press, Oxford).

McDowell, J. 1994. *Mind and World* (Harvard University Press, Cambridge, Ma.).

Moore, G. E. 1959. *Philosophical Papers* (George Allen and Unwin, Ltd., NY).

Moran, R. 2001. *Authority and Estrangement: An Essay on Self-Knowledge* (Princeton University Press, Princeton, NJ).

Nagel, T. 1970. *The Possibility of Altruism* (Princeton University Press, Princeton, N.J.).

—— 1979. *Mortal Questions* (Cambridge University Press, London).

—— 1986. *The View From Nowhere* (Oxford University Press, NY).

—— 1997. *The Last Word* (Oxford University Press, NY).

Nozick, R. 1981. *Philosophical Explanations* (Oxford University Press, Oxford).

Oates, W. J. ed. 1940. *The Stoic and Epicurean Philosophers* (New York: The Modern Library).

Parfit, D. 1986. *Reasons and Persons* (Oxford University Press, NY).

Pascal, B. 1672. *Thoughts* (P. F. Collier and Son, NY [1910]).

Perry, J. 1993. *The Problem of the Essential Indexical and Other Essays* (Oxford University Press, Oxford).

Plantinga, A. 1967. *God and Other Minds: A Study of the Rational Justification of Belief in God* (Cornell University Press, Ithaca, NY).

Pollock, J. 1986. *Contemporary Theories of Knowledge* (Rowman and Littlefield Publishers, Towota, NJ).

Pryor, J. 2000. "The Skeptic and the Dogmatist," *Nous* 34, 4 517–49.

—— 2001. "Highlights of Recent Epistemology," *British Journal of Philosophy of Science* 52, 95–124.

—— 2004. "What's Wrong With Moore's Argument?" *Philosophical Issues* 14, 349–78.

Putnam, H. 1981. *Reason, Truth, and History* (Cambridge University Press, London).

Sartre, J. 1965 (originally published 1946). *Anti-Semite and Jew* (Schocken, NY).

—— 1966 (originally published 1943). *Being and Nothingness* (Washington Square Press, NY).

Schaffer, J. 2005. "Contrastive Knowledge" in *Oxford Studies in Epistemology 1*, eds. T.S. Gendler and J. Hawthorne, 235–71.

Searle, J. 1983. *Intentionality: An Essay in the Philosophy of Mind* (Cambridge University Press, Cambridge).

Siegel, S. 2010. *The Contents of Visual Experience* (Oxford University Press, NY).

Sosa, E. 2007. *A Virtue Epistemology: Apt Belief and Reflective Knowledge* (Oxford University Press, NY).

Spinoza, B. 1919 (originally published 1677). *Ethics*, translated by R. H. M. Elwes (Bell Publishing, London).

Stanley, J. 2008. "Knowledge and Certainty," *Philosophical Issues* 18, 35–57.

Strawson, P. F. 1985. *Skepticism and Naturalism: Some Varieties* (Columbia University Press, NY).

Stroud, B. 1984. *The Significance of Philosophical Scepticism* (Oxford University Press, NY).

Tice, M. and Wallace, H. M. 2003. "The Reflected Self: Creating Yourself as (You Think) Others See You," in M. R. Leary and J. P. Tangey, eds., *Handbook of Self and Identity* (The Guilford Press, NY), pp. 91–106.

de Unamuno, M. 1962 (originally published 1912). *The Tragic Sense of Life* (The Fontana Library, NY).

Watson, G. 1982. "Free Agency," in G. Watson, ed., *Free Will* (Oxford University Press, NY).

White, R. 2006. "Problems for Dogmatism," *Philosophical Studies* 131, 525–57.

Williams, B. 1982. *The New York Review of Books*, Vol. 29, No. 2.

Williamson, T. 2000. *Knowledge and Its Limits* (Oxford University Press, Oxford).

—— 2007. *The Philosophy of Philosophy* (Blackwell, Oxford).

Wittgenstein, L. 1953. *Philosophical Investigations* (Blackwell, Oxford).

—— 1969. *On Certainty* (Blackwell, Oxford).

Wright, C. 2004. "Warrant for Nothing (And Foundations for Free)," *Aristotelian Society Supplement* 78, 167–212.

Yourgrau, P. 1982. "Frege, Perry, and Demonstratives," *The Canadian Journal of Philosophy*, Vol. XII, No. 4.

INDEX

Adler, Jonathan 43–4
agent-relative and agent-neutral
    principles 135
alief 206 n.34
aloneness *see* loneliness
Alston, William 100
altruism, doubt and 22–5
animals 165, 179, 189–90, 211–12, 214
anxiety 3–4, 6, 18, 20–1, 47, 206–7,
    215–17
    probability and 48–9, 60
    see also doubt
Apikoros 149
ashirim 55–6
Austin, J. L. 114, 219

backwards causality 5
Bayesian analysis 41, 110, 135–8
Beckett, Samuel 23, 61, 63–4
    Waiting for Godot 51–2, 53, 59, 176
behaviorism 105
Beis Hamedrish 148
belief(s)
    about other people's experience 135
    autobiographical 192–3
    certainty and 35–46, 196
    control and 156
    delusional circumstances and 115
    doubt and 35–6, 203–9
    emotions and 174–5
    reason and 20, 33–4, 140–2
    reasons for 30–1, 33–5, 50–1, 140
    safety condition 78, 83, 132
    whether immune from revision 153
    whether one identifies with 203–9

Berkeley, George 104, 144 n.2
brain in a vat *see* vat-person
Bratman, Michael 165, 199–202
Broughton, Janet 28, 200, 203–9

Camus, Albert 55
carelessness 33
caring 154
Cartesian reflection 6–13, 17, 147,
    149–50, 151, 155
    see also Descartes
causality 5
certainty, belief and 35–46, 196
Chafetz Chaim 151
children 23, 83, 165, 212
chiluk 94, 97
Chumash 151
comedy 63–4
comparisons 181–6, 196–8
conflicting attitudes 203–9
consciousness 164
    sub-rational level of 213–18
    see also animals
context 32–3 n.24, 45–6
control, belief/doubt and 156

death 6, 29–30, 150, 218
decision-making 162
defeasibility 91, 100–7, 132–3
delusions and delusional circumstances
    101–11, 115, 117–21, 132–40
    see also dreams
demon, Descartes' 6
Descartes, René 6–13 n.2, 17, 37,
    48–9, 85, 119, 139, 159, 162

desire(s) 157, 164–6, 199–203,
    209
  reflective 154, 165, 199–200;
    see also love
Dicker, Georges 160
disagreement 133–5
dishonesty 29
disjunctivism 87–8
diyuk 44
doubt 128, 211–12
  altruism and 22–5
  anxiety and 8–11, 13–14, 20–1,
    28–32, 49, 150
  belief(s) and 35–6, 203–9
  control and 156
  evidence and 128, 131–3, 205
  human nature and 19, 210
  past/present/future and 77, 80–1,
    120, 127–8, 131–3
  reasons for 30–1, 33–5, 124–8,
    138–40
  shadow of 213–18
  strong and weak senses 35–6
  whether one identifies with 203–9
  whether philosophical level
    possible 204–9
  whether possible 8–9, 11, 13–14,
    18–21, 27–8, 30, 150, 152; two-
    level view 28–9, 200, 203–9,
    213–18
  see also anxiety, external
    reality, one-/two-level
    cases concerning trusting
    experience *and under* Vatol
dreams 111–19, 121–2, 144–5
  see also delusions

Egan, Andy 110
Ein mearvin simcha be-simcha
  7, 142
eitzah 129
Elga, Adam 110

envy 55–6
Epicurus 29
epistemic anxiety *see* anxiety *and*
  doubt
epistemic principles and perceptual
  experience *see* perceptual
  primciples
epistemic reasons for belief 30, 31,
  33, 140
  see also belief(s)
evidence
  doubt and *see under* doubt
  for past, present or future
    existence of vat-people 127–8,
    131–3
  Talmudic principles 94–5
existence, basic framework of 152
external reality, doubting 3, 22–5, 54,
  147, 153
  imagining 162–3
  valuing and 154–5, 158–71
  whether possible 35, 155, 158–9,
    172–4, 203–19
  while believing in it 203–9
  see also doubt, perceptual principles
    and sense experience
eye-drops example *see* two-level cases
  concerning trusting experience

faith *see under* religion
Fantl, Jeremy 33
fear *see* anxiety
Feyerabend, Paul 6, 65
Feynman, Richard 5
framework of existence, basic 152
Frankfurt, Harry 153–4, 157, 162,
  165, 198–203

Gemara *see* Talmud and Talmudic
  references
Gendler, Tamar 206 n.34
God 12–13, 148–9, 151

hakchashah 97–9
halachah 5, 7, 94–5, 97–9, 106–7, 128, 142, 197
hallucinations and delusional circumstances 101–11, 115, 117–21, 135–8
  see also dreams
ha-peh she-asar/ha-peh she-hitir 106–7
Hawthorne, John 93
hazamah 97–9
healthy minds *see* sanity
heap, paradox of *see* sorites
hineni 68
hinge propositions 152, 173
human nature
  and doubt 19, 210
  reason and 9, 139
Hume, David 8 n.3, 9, 11, 18–19, 28, 48–9, 139, 140, 180 n.19, 203–10

identification 154, 198–209
  see also self
ikar ha-lashon 42
impossibility/possibility of doubt
  see under doubt (whether possible) *and under* external reality, doubting (whether possible)
inattention 33
insanity *see under* sanity
intellectual responsibility 155–62, 179, 194, 209–17
intention, belief and 31
intentionalist analysis of perception 86
interaction
  doubting 3; *see also* external reality, doubting
  and valuing one's life 155, 158–76
  see also loneliness
irony 58–63

James, William 11–12, 88–9, 174–5
Johnson, Samuel 144 n.2
judgment(s)
  delusional circumstances and 115
  foundation of 152
  of value 164–5

Kabbalah 12
Kagan, Yisrael Meir 151
Kant, Immanuel 172–6
Kaplan, David 193
Kelly, Thomas 132 n.22
kiblu chazal 176
kinas sofrim 55–6, 65
knowledge 219
  anxiety concerning 20
  faith and 50
  see also evidence
Korsgaard, Christine 187
Kotler, Aharon 176
Kripke, Saul 32, 34, 96, 105, 193

la-afukei 44
language games 174, 176
languages 42
lashon hakodesh 42
lech lecha 215
le-chumra 107
Leite, Adam 108, 114
le-kula 107
life, valuing one's 155, 158–76
lo ba-shamayim hi 187
Locke, John 116
logical form 87–8
logical models 95–6
loneliness 147–8, 150
  of vat-people 6–7
  see also solitude
loops 107–18, 132–3, 138
  see also dreams

love 153–4, 174, 202–3
  see also reflective desire
lucidity, dreaming and 114–17

madness *see under* sanity
Martin, Michael 87
Marušić, Berislav 31, 49–50
Matrix, the 103–4, 124, 127
McDowell, John 87
McGrath, Matthew 33
meaning 153, 160–1
  see also valuing
mefarshim 97
memory 110, 141–2
mesirus nefesh 61
Mishnah *see* Talmud and Talmudic
  references
modeling 95–6
Moore, G. E. 24, 37, 56–7, 111–13

nachas 80
Nagel, Thomas 6, 8, 9, 19, 28, 55–62,
  135 n.23, 140, 200, 204–5, 217
non-circularity principle 100–10, 111,
  118, 132–3
  see also loops
Nozick, Robert 34
n-to-n+1 argument 70–80, 84,
  132–3

one-/two-level cases concerning
  trusting experience 90–4,
  97–103, 105–7, 111–12,
  119–20, 133
other minds/lives/people 149, 155, 158
  experience, beliefs about 135
  and valuing one's life 158–76
  see also external reality

palginan dibura 106
paradoxes 20–1, 37, 74
  see also sorites *and* uncertainty

Parfit, Derek 186–8
past/present/future
  doubt and 77, 80–1, 120, 127–8,
    131–3
  self and 186, 189
perception
  disagreement and 133–5
  memory and 141–2
  reason and 141–2
  see also sense experience
perceptual principles (epistemic
  principles and perceptual
  experience) 83–9, 115, 132–3,
  138
  non-circularity principle and
    loops 100–10, 111, 118, 132–3
  one-/two-level cases 90–4, 97–103,
    105–7, 111–12, 119–20, 132–3
Perry, John 193
phenomenal force 86–7, 88–9
Piaget, Jean 212
Plantinga, Alvin 149
Plato 66, 83
ployderer 149
Ployderville 108–11
Pollock, John 90 n.9
possibility/impossibility of doubt
  see under doubt (whether
    possible) *and under* external
    reality, doubting (whether
    possible)
pragmatic reasons for belief 30–1
  see also belief(s)
presence, sense of 88–9
pride 180 n.19, 181–6, 196–8
principles
  reasoning and 100, 135
  see also perceptual principles
probability 93–5, 135–8
  anxiety and 48–9, 60
  of future existence of vat-people
    127–8

loops and 110
and trusting sense-experiences 92–3
valuing and 169–71
see also seriousness
propositional content 86
Pryor, James 85–9, 111–13, 117, 132
psychology 210
see also human nature
Purim 208
Putnam, Hilary 31–2, 104

Quine, Willard Van Orman 153

rabbinical training 129
radical skepticism *see* doubt
Rashba 42
reality
external *see* external reality
sense of 88–9
reason 139–42, 155–8, 161–2
and beliefs 20, 33–4, 140–2
and doubt 18–21
human nature and 9, 139
reasoning 100, 135
responsible 155–62, 179, 194, 209–17
reasons *see under* belief(s), *under* doubt *and under* Vatol
reflectiveness and reflective desire 154, 165, 199–203
see also love
religion and religious faith 50, 148–9, 150–1
see also Talmud
responsibility, intellectual 155–62, 179, 194, 209–17
rov 94
ruba d'eesa kaman/ruba d'lessa kaman 94–5
Russell, Bertrand 24, 46, 50

safek 128
safety condition 78, 83, 132
sanity and insanity 6–10, 11–12, 54, 147, 150–1, 155, 218
Sartre, Jean-Paul 66, 180, 208
Schoenfeld, Miriam 135–8
Searle, John 86
Seder 103
self 179–203
self-deception 206, 208–9, 213–17, 219
see also wishful thinking
self-esteem 46, 179–88, 194, 195–8
sense experience 84–9, 115
delusion and 119, 132–5, 138–40
non-circularity principle and loops 100–10, 111, 132–3
one-/two-level cases concerning trusting 90–4, 97–103, 105–7, 111–12, 119–20, 133
other people's 135
see also external reality
seriousness 54, 62, 90
see also probability
sevara 94, 129
sfek sfekah 128
shiur 176
Shlomo ben Aderet (Rashba) 42
sick soul *see under* sanity
Siegel, Susanna 86
Simchas Torah 208
skepticism *see* doubt
Socrates 66
sofrim 55–6, 65
solipsism 144, 168–9
solitude and solitary beings 160–7, 168–71, 179–81, 184–6, 194–5
see also loneliness
sorites 21, 70–7
Sosa, Ernest 20, 111 n.17
Spinoza, Baruch 187
standards *see* comparisons

Strawson, Peter 9, 28, 200, 204–5
Stroud, Barry 50, 62, 141
stupidity 29
sub-rational level of consciousness
213–18
sugyah 148

taiku 142
Talmud and Talmudic references 5, 7,
13, 58, 94–5, 97–9, 106–7, 128,
142, 148–9, 151, 176, 194, 197,
215–16
Talmudic inference 44
tefillin 151, 176–8
tenai le-mafrea 5
tenses 121
see also past/present/future
thought experiments 14–19, 162–4
see also vat-people
Torah *see* Talmud
tragedy 217–18
translations 9 n.1
two-level cases concerning trusting
experience 90–4, 97–103,
105–7, 111–12, 119–20, 133
two-level view of doubt 28–9, 200

Unamuno, Miguel de 140
uncertainty 35–46
unfathomable solitude 160, 166
see also solitude

valuing 154–5, 158–76
see also self-esteem
Vatol 14–20
level of doubt 28–9
and loops 118, 138
rationality of anxiety 47
rationality of doubt that he is a
vat-person 15, 21–2, 30–1, 48,
70–80, 89–90, 103, 110, 120,
133–5

reasons to believe that he is not
a vat-person 104, 105, 120,
123–6
and uncertainty 36–8
whether doubt possible for
211–19
whether position different from
ours 124–6, 132 n.22, 136–40,
142, 218–19
see also doubt *and* vat-people
vat-person/vat-people 14–19, 121–4
belief concerning whether being
34–5, 48–9
communication as issue 104
evidence for past, present or
future existence 127–8, 131–3
rationality of belief in possibility
of being 127–8, 132–3
values and subjective states
167–8
see also loneliness *and* Vatol
virtue 150

Waiting for Godot see under Beckett
wantonness 157, 162, 165, 212
Watson, Gary 165 n.10
White, Roger 86, 112
Williams, Bernard 34
Williamson, Timothy 12, 22–5, 36–7,
40, 49, 71, 126
wishful thinking 174–5
see also self-deception
witnesses 97–9
Wittgenstein, Ludwig 8, 9, 56, 87,
104–5, 148, 152–3, 172–4, 193,
202

yagdil Torah ve-yadir 194
Yeshivas 148
Yourgrau, Palle 193

Zeh neheneh ve-zehlo chaser 197